# The New York Times

IN THE HEADLINES

# Identity Politics

THE NEW YORK TIMES EDITORIAL STAFF

Published in 2019 by The New York Times® Educational Publishing
in association with The Rosen Publishing Group, Inc.
29 East 21st Street, New York, NY 10010

First Edition

**The New York Times**
Alex Ward: Editorial Director, Book Development
Phyllis Collazo: Photo Rights/Permissions Editor
Heidi Giovine: Administrative Manager

**Rosen Publishing**
Megan Kellerman: Managing Editor
Elizabeth Schmermund: Editor
Greg Tucker: Creative Director
Brian Garvey: Art Director

**Cataloging-in-Publication Data**
Names: New York Times Company.
Title: Identity politics / edited by the New York Times editorial staff.
Description: New York : New York Times Educational Publishing,
2019. | Series: In the headlines | Includes glossary and index.
Identifiers: ISBN 9781642821215 (library bound) | ISBN
9781642821208 (pbk.) | ISBN 9781642821222 (ebook)
Subjects: LCSH: Political culture—United States—Juvenile
literature. | Identity politics—United States—Juvenile literature. |
Group identity—Political aspects—United States—Juvenile literature.
Classification: LCC JK1726.I346 2019 | DDC 306.2—dc23

*Manufactured in the United States of America*

**On the cover:** Artwork by Dan Gluibizzi.

# Contents

**CHAPTER 3**

# Race and Representation in Media

**CHAPTER 4**

# The Alt-Right and White Identity

**CHAPTER 5**

# Feminism and LGBTQ Rights

# Introduction

IDENTITY POLITICS — in which groups of people who share an aspect of their identity promote their own interests over others' interests — helps people understand the world and their place in it, but it has also led to racism, sexism and bigotry. Identity politics has been put to great use in the fight for both civil rights and women's rights in the United States, where African-Americans and women politically organized around the injustices and needs of their racial and gender identities. Since the late 1960s and 1970s, modern society's relationship with identity politics has gone through many changes. Today, many people recognize that there is not one particular facet of our identities that dictates the rest; rather, we are all made up of an intricate web of different identities, all of which make us both absolutely unique and perhaps more able to relate to the uniqueness of others. For example, an African-American woman's identity is not only informed by her gender and racial identities, but also by her socioeconomic background, her religious upbringing and her unique experiences. Identity is not a monolithic thing, after all.

While many politicians and analysts have lauded identity politics for its ability to bring the voices of marginalized peoples to the forefront, it has also been criticized for its inherent divisiveness. The cacophony surrounding identity politics has only become louder in recent years with the polarization of contemporary politics. In the United States, much attention has been paid to President Donald Trump's use of an identity politics based on white, working-class identity, which secured him the presidency in the fall of 2016. Some argue that the failure of identity politics led to this divisive election, while others argue that identity politics is the only thing that can "fix"

Donald Trump's 2016 campaign set in motion a process that reoriented American politics toward the cosmopolitanism versus nationalism divide that he has emphasized.

rampant racism and sexism — even as it is being used on the extreme right to quell marginalized voices.

The articles in this collection examine identity politics from various angles, all within the pages of The New York Times and involving contemporary debates — examining its impact on elections, race, the representation of people in media, LGBTQ rights, feminism and more. There's no clear-cut solution to the role identity politics should play in modern culture, precisely because it is such an ingrained part of the human condition. But these articles can help elucidate the role of identity politics in both larger political and world events, and in our own lives.

# CHAPTER 1

# What Is Identity Politics?

The articles collected in this chapter examine how identity politics has been used in the recent past and our contemporary moment. They probe general questions about the political usefulness of identity politics and how a focus on the politics of identity affects the way we live — and create art — in our world. The chapter starts with a well-known and oft-criticized analysis by Professor Mark Lilla of why the end of identity politics, or identity liberalism, must and will occur — and what a post-identity politics world might look like.

## The End of Identity Liberalism

**OPINION | BY MARK LILLA | NOV. 18, 2016**

IT IS A TRUISM that America has become a more diverse country. It is also a beautiful thing to watch. Visitors from other countries, particularly those having trouble incorporating different ethnic groups and faiths, are amazed that we manage to pull it off. Not perfectly, of course, but certainly better than any European or Asian nation today. It's an extraordinary success story.

But how should this diversity shape our politics? The standard liberal answer for nearly a generation now has been that we should become aware of and "celebrate" our differences. Which is a splendid principle of moral pedagogy — but disastrous as a foundation for democratic politics in our ideological age. In recent years American liberalism has slipped into a kind of moral panic about racial, gender and sexual identity that has distorted liberalism's message and prevented it from becoming a unifying force capable of governing.

One of the many lessons of the recent presidential election campaign and its repugnant outcome is that the age of identity liberalism must be brought to an end. Hillary Clinton was at her best and most uplifting when she spoke about American interests in world affairs and how they relate to our understanding of democracy. But when it came to life at home, she tended on the campaign trail to lose that large vision and slip into the rhetoric of diversity, calling out explicitly to African-American, Latino, L.G.B.T. and women voters at every stop. This was a strategic mistake. If you are going to mention groups in America, you had better mention all of them. If you don't, those left out will notice and feel excluded. Which, as the data show, was exactly what happened with the white working class and those with strong religious convictions. Fully two-thirds of white voters without college degrees voted for Donald Trump, as did over 80 percent of white evangelicals.

The moral energy surrounding identity has, of course, had many good effects. Affirmative action has reshaped and improved corporate life. Black Lives Matter has delivered a wake-up call to every American with a conscience. Hollywood's efforts to normalize homosexuality in our popular culture helped to normalize it in American families and public life.

But the fixation on diversity in our schools and in the press has produced a generation of liberals and progressives narcissistically unaware of conditions outside their self-defined groups, and indifferent to the task of reaching out to Americans in every walk of life. At a very young age our children are being encouraged to talk about their individual identities, even before they have them. By the time they reach college many assume that diversity discourse exhausts political discourse, and have shockingly little to say about such perennial questions as class, war, the economy and the common good. In large part this is because of high school history curriculums, which anachronistically project the identity politics of today back onto the past, creating a distorted picture of the major forces and individuals that shaped our country. (The achievements of women's rights movements, for instance, were real and important, but you cannot understand them if you do not first understand the founding fathers' achievement in establishing a system of government based on the guarantee of rights.)

When young people arrive at college they are encouraged to keep this focus on themselves by student groups, faculty members and also administrators whose full-time job is to deal with — and heighten the significance of — "diversity issues." Fox News and other conservative media outlets make great sport of mocking the "campus craziness" that surrounds such issues, and more often than not they are right to. Which only plays into the hands of populist demagogues who want to delegitimize learning in the eyes of those who have never set foot on a campus. How to explain to the average voter the supposed moral urgency of giving college students the right to choose the designated gender pronouns to be used when addressing them? How not to laugh along with those voters at the story of a University of Michigan prankster who wrote in "His Majesty"?

This campus-diversity consciousness has over the years filtered into the liberal media, and not subtly. Affirmative action for women and minorities at America's newspapers and broadcasters has been an extraordinary social achievement — and has even changed, quite literally, the face of right-wing media, as journalists like Megyn Kelly and Laura Ingraham have gained prominence. But it also appears to have encouraged the assumption, especially among younger journalists and editors, that simply by focusing on identity they have done their jobs.

Recently I performed a little experiment during a sabbatical in France: For a full year I read only European publications, not American ones. My thought was to try seeing the world as European readers did. But it was far more instructive to return home and realize how the lens of identity has transformed American reporting in recent years. How often, for example, the laziest story in American journalism — about the "first X to do Y" — is told and retold. Fascination with the identity drama has even affected foreign reporting, which is in distressingly short supply. However interesting it may be to read, say, about the fate of transgender people in Egypt, it contributes nothing to educating Americans about the powerful political and religious currents that will determine Egypt's future, and indirectly, our own. No major news outlet in Europe would think of adopting such a focus.

But it is at the level of electoral politics that identity liberalism has failed most spectacularly, as we have just seen. National politics in healthy periods is not about "difference," it is about commonality. And it will be dominated by whoever best captures Americans' imaginations about our shared destiny. Ronald Reagan did that very skillfully, whatever one may think of his vision. So did Bill Clinton, who took a page from Reagan's playbook. He seized the Democratic Party away from its identity-conscious wing, concentrated his energies on domestic programs that would benefit everyone (like national health insurance) and defined America's role in the post-1989 world. By remaining in office for two terms, he was then able to accomplish much for different groups in the Democratic coalition. Identity politics, by contrast, is largely expressive, not persuasive. Which is why it never wins elections — but can lose them.

The media's newfound, almost anthropological, interest in the angry white male reveals as much about the state of our liberalism as it does about this much maligned, and previously ignored, figure. A convenient liberal interpretation of the recent presidential election would have it that Mr. Trump won in large part because he managed to transform economic disadvantage into racial rage — the "whitelash" thesis. This is convenient because it sanctions a conviction of moral superiority and allows liberals to ignore what those voters said were their overriding concerns. It also encourages the fantasy that the Republican right is doomed to demographic extinction in the long run —

which means liberals have only to wait for the country to fall into their laps. The surprisingly high percentage of the Latino vote that went to Mr. Trump should remind us that the longer ethnic groups are here in this country, the more politically diverse they become.

Finally, the whitelash thesis is convenient because it absolves liberals of not recognizing how their own obsession with diversity has encouraged white, rural, religious Americans to think of themselves as a disadvantaged group whose identity is being threatened or ignored. Such people are not actually reacting against the reality of our diverse America (they tend, after all, to live in homogeneous areas of the country). But they are reacting against the omnipresent rhetoric of identity, which is what they mean by "political correctness." Liberals should bear in mind that the first identity movement in American politics was the Ku Klux Klan, which still exists. Those who play the identity game should be prepared to lose it.

We need a post-identity liberalism, and it should draw from the past successes of pre-identity liberalism. Such a liberalism would concentrate on widening its base by appealing to Americans as Americans and emphasizing the issues that affect a vast majority of them. It would speak to the nation as a nation of citizens who are in this together and must help one another. As for narrower issues that are highly charged symbolically and can drive potential allies away, especially those touching on sexuality and religion, such a liberalism would work quietly, sensitively and with a proper sense of scale. (To paraphrase Bernie Sanders, America is sick and tired of hearing about liberals' damn bathrooms.)

Teachers committed to such a liberalism would refocus attention on their main political responsibility in a democracy: to form committed citizens aware of their system of government and the major forces and events in our history. A post-identity liberalism would also emphasize that democracy is not only about rights; it also confers duties on its citizens, such as the duties to keep informed and vote. A post-identity liberal press would begin educating itself about parts of the country that have been ignored, and about what matters there, especially religion. And it would take seriously its responsibility to educate Americans about the major forces shaping world politics, especially their historical dimension.

Some years ago I was invited to a union convention in Florida to speak on a panel about Franklin D. Roosevelt's famous Four Freedoms speech of 1941. The hall was full of representatives from local chapters — men, women, blacks, whites, Latinos. We began by singing the national anthem, and then sat down to listen to a recording of Roosevelt's speech. As I looked out into the crowd, and saw the array of different faces, I was struck by how focused they were on what they shared. And listening to Roosevelt's stirring voice as he invoked the freedom of speech, the freedom of worship, the freedom from want and the freedom from fear — freedoms that Roosevelt demanded for "everyone in the world" — I was reminded of what the real foundations of modern American liberalism are.

MARK LILLA, a professor of the humanities at Columbia and a visiting scholar at the Russell Sage Foundation, is the author, most recently, of "The Shipwrecked Mind: On Political Reaction."

# Identity Politics and Its Defenders

OPINION | BY DAVID LEONHARDT | NOV. 21, 2016

MARK LILLA'S MUCH-DISCUSSED PIECE in yesterday's Times tapped into a debate about "identity politics." Lilla argued that Democrats had lost the election by focusing on ethnicity, gender and sexuality rather than "appealing to Americans as Americans and emphasizing the issues that affect a vast majority of them."

His view fits with the post-election conventional wisdom: that Democrats must do better appealing to the white working class to regain power. I largely agree, but I also think that Democrats need to be careful about alienating their current constituencies — particularly since many of those constituencies are growing.

So I spent some time yesterday looking for critiques of Lilla, to think through their arguments.

The core criticism was that Lilla was wrong to suggest the political left deserves blame for initiating the focus on racial (and other) groups. "The label of 'identity politics' is mostly ridiculous whenever used, because American politics historically was based on white male identity," Vann R. Newkirk II of The Atlantic wrote on Twitter. "Trump's entire candidacy & now presidency was based on one of the most effective campaigns of identity politics in history."

Likewise, Ira Madison III, at MTV.com, wrote: "Trump is confirming racists and white nationalists for his cabinet, but it's the liberals focusing on identity politics that are getting us into trouble?"

All of these arguments make a vital historical point: This country's deep racial problems stem from discrimination, not from oversensitivity about discrimination. And it would be a terrible mistake for anyone to shy away from criticizing Donald Trump's alarming choices for attorney general and chief White House strategist.

At the same time, there's a reality that Democrats would be foolish to underestimate. This country's political system — the rules for

Delegates listened as Hillary Clinton spoke in July, at the Democratic National Convention.

electing both Congress and the president — is biased toward large, sparsely populated areas. Those areas tend to be overwhelmingly white.

Unless Democrats can win more support from white voters than they did this year, the party will be left to complain about the country's political situation rather than do something about it.

**DAVID LEONHARDT** is an Op-Ed columnist and associate editorial page editor at The New York Times.

# Who Gets to Write What

OPINION  |  BY KAITLYN GREENIDGE  |  SEPT. 24, 2016

WHEN I WAS in graduate school, I remember a fellow writer bringing to a workshop a lynching scene. The writer was not black. He was, in fact, a Chinese-American man named Bill Cheng, who would go on to write a novel of the blues called "Southern Cross the Dog."

In class that day, we hemmed and hawed over discussing the scene until our professor slammed the table and shouted at the room, "Does Bill have the right to write this scene?"

"No," one of my classmates answered, one of the other writers of color in the room, who was also, like Bill, not black. I remember being furious, spitting mad. Of course, of course, I thought, he has a right to write this scene. At the time, I don't think I could have said why I felt so strongly, was so offended by the fact that our white professor would ask this of a room of mixed writers.

Now I look back and I can say I felt so strongly that Bill had a right to write that scene because he wrote it well. Because he was a good writer, a thoughtful writer, and that scene had a reason to exist besides morbid curiosity or a petulant delight in shrugging on and off another's pain — the fact that a reader couldn't see that shook my core about what fiction could and couldn't do.

And yet the question was worth asking: Had he "culturally appropriated" an experience — an experience of pain, no less? He hadn't been lynched, and when most people think of lynching in this country, they do not think of people who look like him. Should everyone get to create the art they feel called to make?

Some would have you believe that if you're a serious writer, you are not allowed to add questions about who is telling what story and why to the list of things we ask of a piece of fiction.

It can be hard to come up with real answers to those questions. It's especially difficult if you aren't doing the work of creating fully human characters, regardless of your or their identity. And it can be really, really, hard to come up against your own blindness, when as a writer, you are supposed to be a great observer. It can be terrifying to come to the realization that it is totally possible to write into this blind spot for years. Whole books, in fact whole genres of fiction, make their home in this blind spot, because of writers' publishing community's biases.

When I was writing my first novel, I was determined to include a section in the voice of an 80-year-old, white, Yankee heiress. The character is deeply racist, but the kind of racist who would consider Donald J. Trump vulgar and never use the ugliest of racial epithets. Bone china and lace tablecloth and genteelly rusted Volvo parked at the family home in Concord, Mass. kind of racist. Her inability to honestly acknowledge her racism leads to her complicity in a large, very awful crime against a community of people, one she spends a chapter of the book attempting to apologize for, without ever admitting guilt. She desperately wishes for black Americans' approval while still being unable to imagine us as humans with a full emotional range like hers.

It was a personality I thought I knew well, growing up going to the prep schools of the wealthy and connected as a scholarship student. I wrote a draft in this voice, tucked it into my manuscript like a stink bomb, and smugly sent it off to my agent and my professor, waiting for their reactions.

"It doesn't work," I was told. "She's not believable as a character. She doesn't work." "Damn white readers," I jokingly said to my friends. But once I got over myself, I took apart that section piece by piece. I rewrote and failed and rewrote and failed. As much as this character had begun as an indictment of all the hypocrisies of my childhood, she was not going to come out on the page that way, not without a lot of work. I was struck by an awful realization. I would have to love this monster into existence. The voice of this character had been full of scorn and condescension. I rewrote it with those elements in place, but covered with the treacly, grasping attempts at affection of a broken and desperately lonely woman.

Five years or so after I came to that realization, I wrote to Bill Cheng after reading the novelist Lionel Shriver's keynote on "Fiction and Identity Politics" at the Brisbane Writer's Festival. Wearing a sombrero, Ms. Shriver spoke out against "cultural appropriation" as a valid critique, arguing that it censored her work as a writer, that she would not have free rein to fully imagine others' perspectives and widen her world of characters. "Did you hear about this?" I typed into our chat window, and Bill wrote back, "Hold on …" Then his answer pinged.

"Why do they want our approval so badly?" Bill typed back to me.

This is the question, of course. It's the wish not so much to be able to write a character of another race, but to do so without criticism. And at the heart of that rather ludicrous request is a question of power. There is the power of rendering another's perspective, which is not your own. There is the adage "Don't punch down," which sits like the shiny red lever of a fire alarm, irresistible for some writers who wish to pull it.

We writers, in the United States at least, have a peculiar, tortured relationship with power. We want it both ways. We talk about the power of the written word to shift whole levels of consciousness while constantly lamenting the death of publishing, the death of the novel, the death of the reader. Those first concerns are valid, but the last become questionable, especially in the face of numerous studies to the contrary that say that people are reading at similar rates as a few years ago. Readership has also grown in certain groups — according to analysis of recent data, the demographic group most likely to have read a book in the last year is college-educated black women.

The anxiety about a shrinking audience is accompanied by a dull realization that writing from the perspectives of those who have traditionally been silenced in "great literature" — the queer, the colored, the poor, the stateless — is being bought, being sold, and most important to writers obsessed with status (and we are all obsessed with status), winning awards and acclaim.

Claudia Rankine, when awarded the MacArthur genius grant this past week, noted that the prize was "the culture saying: We have an investment in dismantling white dominance in our culture. If you're trying to do that, we're going to help you." For some, this sounds exciting. For others, this reads as a threat — at best, a suggestion to catch up and engage with a subject, race, that for a long time has been thought of as not "universal," not "deep" enough for fiction. The panic around all of this is driving these outbursts.

It must feel like a reversal of fate to those who have not been paying attention. The other, who has been relegated to the background character, wise outcast, dash of magic, or terror or cool or symbolism, or more simply emotional or physical whore, is expected to be the main event, and some writers suspect that they may not be up for that challenge.

A writer has the right to inhabit any character she pleases — she's always had it and will continue to have it. The complaint seems to be less that some people ask writers to think about cultural appropriation, and more that a writer wishes her work not to be critiqued for doing so, that instead she get a gold star for trying.

Whenever I hear this complaint, I am reminded of Toni Morrison's cool assessment of "anti-P.C. backlash" more than 20 years ago: "What I think the political correctness debate is really about is the power to be able to define. The definers want the power to name. And the defined are now taking that power away from them."

The quote is two decades old, but this debate, in certain circles, has never moved past the paranoia about nonexistent censorship.

This debate, or rather, this level of the debate, is had over and over again, primarily because of an unwillingness on one side to consider history or even entertain a long line of arguments in response. Instead, what often happens is a writer or artist acts as though she is taking some brave stand by declaring to be against political correctness. As if our entire culture is not already centered on a very particular version of whiteness that many white people don't even inhabit anymore. And so, someone makes a comment or a statement without nuance or sense of history, only with an implicit insistence that writing and publishing magically exist outside the structures of power that dominate every other aspect of our daily lives.

Imagine the better, stronger fiction that could be produced if writers took this challenge to stretch and grow one's imagination, to afford the same depth of humanity and interest and nuance to characters who look like them as characters who don't, to take those stories seriously and actually think about power when writing — how much further fiction could go as an art.

It's the difference between a child playing dress-up in a costume for the afternoon and someone putting on a set of clothes and going to work.

**KAITLYN GREENIDGE** (@kkgreenidge) is the author of the novel "We Love You, Charlie Freeman."

# Will the Left Survive the Millennials?

OPINION  |  BY LIONEL SHRIVER  |  SEPT. 23, 2016

MIDWAY THROUGH MY opening address for the Brisbane Writers Festival earlier this month, Yassmin Abdel-Magied, a Sudanese-born Australian engineer and 25-year-old memoirist, walked out. Her indignant comments about the event might have sunk into obscurity, along with my speech, had they not been republished by The Guardian. Twenty minutes in, this audience member apparently turned to her mother: " 'Mama, I can't sit here,' I said, the corners of my mouth dragging downwards. 'I cannot legitimize this.' " She continued: "The faces around me blurred. As my heels thudded against the grey plastic of the flooring, harmonizing with the beat of the adrenaline pumping through my veins, my mind was blank save for one question. 'How is this happening?' "

I'm asking the same thing.

BENOIT TARDIF

Briefly, my address maintained that fiction writers should be allowed to write fiction — thus should not let concerns about "cultural appropriation" constrain our creation of characters from different backgrounds than our own. I defended fiction as a vital vehicle for empathy. If we have permission to write only about our own personal experience, there is no fiction, but only memoir. Honestly, my thesis seemed so self-evident that I'd worried the speech would be bland.

Nope — not in the topsy-turvy universe of identity politics. The festival immediately disavowed the address, though the organizers had approved the thrust of the talk in advance. A "Right of Reply" session was hastily organized. When, days later, The Guardian ran the speech, social media went ballistic. Mainstream articles followed suit. I plan on printing out The New Republic's "Lionel Shriver Shouldn't Write About Minorities" and taping it above my desk as a chiding reminder.

Viewing the world and the self through the prism of advantaged and disadvantaged groups, the identity-politics movement — in which behavior like huffing out of speeches and stirring up online mobs is par for the course — is an assertion of generational power. Among millennials and those coming of age behind them, the race is on to see who can be more righteous and aggrieved — who can replace the boring old civil rights generation with a spikier brand.

When I was growing up in the '60s and early '70s, conservatives were the enforcers of conformity. It was the right that was suspicious, sniffing out Communists and scrutinizing public figures for signs of sedition.

Now the role of oppressor has passed to the left. In Australia, where I spoke, Section 18C of the Racial Discrimination Act makes it unlawful to do or say anything likely to "offend, insult, humiliate or intimidate," providing alarming latitude in the restriction of free speech. It is Australia's conservatives arguing for the amendment of this law.

As a lifelong Democratic voter, I'm dismayed by the radical left's ever-growing list of dos and don'ts — by its impulse to control, to instill self-censorship as well as to promote real censorship, and to deploy sensitivity as an excuse to be brutally insensitive to any perceived enemy. There are many people who see these frenzies about cultural appropriation, trigger warnings, micro-aggressions and safe spaces as overtly crazy. The shrill tyranny of the left helps to push them toward Donald Trump.

Ironically, only fellow liberals will be cowed by terror of being branded a racist (a pejorative lobbed at me in recent days — one that, however groundless, tends to stick). But there's still such a thing as a real bigot, and a real misogynist. In obsessing over micro-aggressions like the sin of uttering the commonplace Americanism "you guys" to mean "you all," activists persecute fellow travelers who already care about equal rights.

Moreover, people who would hamper free speech always assume that they're designing a world in which only their enemies will have to shut up. But free speech is fragile. Left-wing activists are just as dependent on permission to speak their minds as their detractors.

In an era of weaponized sensitivity, participation in public discourse is growing so perilous, so fraught with the danger of being caught out for using the wrong word or failing to uphold the latest orthodoxy in relation to disability, sexual orientation, economic class, race or ethnicity, that many are apt to bow out. Perhaps intimidating their elders into silence is the intention of the identity-politics cabal — and maybe my generation should retreat to our living rooms and let the young people tear one another apart over who seemed to imply that Asians are good at math.

But do we really want every intellectual conversation to be scrupulously cleansed of any whiff of controversy? Will people, so worried about inadvertently giving offense, avoid those with different backgrounds altogether? Is that the kind of fiction we want — in which the novels of white writers all depict John Cheever's homogeneous Connecticut suburbs of the 1950s, while the real world outside their covers becomes ever more diverse?

Ms. Abdel-Magied got the question right: *How is this happening?* How did the left in the West come to embrace restriction, censorship and the imposition of an orthodoxy at least as tyrannical as the anti-Communist, pro-Christian conformism I grew up with? Liberals have ominously relabeled themselves "progressives," forsaking a noun that had its roots in "liber," meaning free. To *progress* is merely to go forward, and you can go forward into a pit.

Protecting freedom of speech involves protecting the voices of people with whom you may violently disagree. In my youth, liberals would defend the right of neo-Nazis to march down Main Street. I cannot imagine anyone on the left making that case today.

**LIONEL SHRIVER** is the author, most recently, of the novel "The Mandibles: A Family, 2029-2047."

# The Identity Politics of Whiteness

ESSAY | BY LAILA LALAMI | NOV. 21, 2016

THREE YEARS AGO, I read "Adventures of Huckleberry Finn" to my daughter. She smiled as she heard about Huck's mischief, his jokes, his dress-up games, but it was his relationship with the runaway slave Jim that intrigued her most. Huck and Jim travel together as Jim seeks his freedom; at times, Huck wrestles with his decision to help. In the end, Tom Sawyer concocts an elaborate scheme for Jim's release.

When we finished the book, my daughter had a question: Why didn't Tom just tell Jim the truth — that Miss Watson had already freed him in her will? She is not alone in asking; scholars have long debated this issue. One answer lies in white identity, which needs black identity in order to define itself, and therefore cannot exist without it.

"Identity" is a vexing word. It is racial or sexual or national or religious or all those things at once. Sometimes it is proudly claimed, other times hidden or denied. But the word is almost never applied to whiteness. Racial identity is taken to be exclusive to people of color: When we speak about race, it is in connection with African-Americans or Latinos or Asians or Native People or some other group that has been designated a minority. "White" is seen as the default, the absence of race. In school curriculums, one month is reserved for the study of black history, while the rest of the year is just plain history; people will tell you they are fans of black or Latin music, but few will claim they love white music.

This year's election has disturbed that silence. The president-elect earned the votes of a majority of white people while running a campaign that explicitly and consistently appealed to white identity and anxiety. At the heart of this anxiety is white people's increasing awareness that they will become a statistical minority in this country within a generation. The paradox is that they have no language to speak about their own identity. "White" is a category that has afforded them an evasion from race, rather than an opportunity to confront it.

In his campaign for the presidency, Donald Trump regularly tied America's problems to others. Immigration must be reformed, he told us, to stop the rapists and drug dealers coming here from Mexico. Terrorism could be stopped by banning Muslims from entering the country. The big banks would not be held in check by his opponent, whose picture he tweeted alongside a Star of David. The only people that the president-elect never faulted for anything were whites. These people he spoke of not as an indistinguishable mass but as a multitude of individuals, victims of a system that was increasingly rigged against them.

A common refrain in the days after the election was "Not all his voters are racist." But this will not do, because those voters chose a candidate who promised them relief from their problems at the expense of other races. They may claim innocence now, but it seems to me that when a leading chapter of the Ku Klux Klan announces plans to hold a victory parade for the president-elect, the time for innocence is long past.

RACISM IS A necessary explanation for what happened on Nov. 8, but it is not a sufficient one. Last February, when the subject of racial identity came up at the Democratic primary debate in Milwaukee, the moderator Gwen Ifill surprised many viewers by asking about white voters: "By the middle of this century, the nation is going to be majority nonwhite," she said. "Our public schools are already there. If working-class white Americans are about to be outnumbered, are already underemployed in many cases, and one study found they are dying sooner, don't they have a reason to be resentful?"

Hillary Clinton said she was concerned about every community, including white communities "where we are seeing an increase in alcoholism, addiction, earlier deaths." She said she planned to revitalize what she called "coal country" and explore spending more in communities with persistent generational poverty. Senator Bernie Sanders took a different view: "We can talk about it as a racial issue," he said. "But it is a general economic issue." Workers of all races, he said, have been hurt by trade deals like Nafta. "We need to start paying attention to the needs of working families in this country."

This resonated with me: I, too, come from the working class, and from the significant portion of it that is not white. Neither of my parents went to college. Still, they managed to put their children through school and buy a home — a life that, for many in the working class, is impossible now. Nine months after that debate, we have found out exactly how much attention we should have been paying such families. The same white working-class voters who re-elected Obama four years ago did not cast their ballots for Clinton this year. These voters suffer from economic disadvantages even as they enjoy racial advantages. But it is impossible for them to notice these racial advantages if they live in rural areas where everyone around them is white. What they perceive instead is the cruel sense of being forgotten by the political class and condescended to by the cultural one.

While poor white voters are being scrutinized now, less attention has been paid to voters who are white and rich. White voters flocked to Trump by a wide margin, and he won a majority of voters who earn more than $50,000 a year, despite their relative economic safety. A majority of white women chose him, too, even though more than a dozen women have accused him of sexual assault. No, the top issue that drove Trump's voters to the polls was not the economy — more voters concerned about that went to Clinton. It was immigration, an issue on which we've abandoned serious debate and become engulfed in sensational stories about rapists crossing the southern border or the pending imposition of Shariah law in the Midwest.

IF WHITENESS IS no longer the default and is to be treated as an identity — even, soon, a "minority" — then perhaps it is time white people considered the disadvantages of being a race. The next time a white man bombs an abortion clinic or goes on a shooting rampage on a college campus, white people might have to be lectured on religious tolerance and called upon to denounce the violent extremists in their midst. The opioid epidemic in today's white communities could be treated the way we once treated the crack epidemic in black ones — not as a failure of the government to take care of its people but as a failure of the race. The fact that this has not happened, nor is it likely to, only serves as evidence that white Americans can still escape race.

Much has been made about privilege in this election. I will readily admit to many privileges. I have employer-provided health care. I live in a nice suburb. I am not dependent on government benefits. But I am also an immigrant and a person of color and a Muslim. On the night of the election, I was away from my family. Speaking to them on the phone, I could hear the terror in my daughter's voice as the returns came in. The next morning, her friends at school, most of them Asian or Jewish or Hispanic, were in tears. My daughter called on the phone. "He can't make us leave, right?" she asked. "We're citizens."

My husband and I did our best to quiet her fears. No, we said. He cannot make us leave. But every time I have thought about this conversation — and I have thought about it dozens of times, in my sleepless nights since the election — I have felt less certain. For all the privileges I can pass on to my daughter, there is one I cannot: whiteness.

LAILA LALAMI is the author, most recently, of "The Moor's Account," a finalist for the Pulitzer Prize for fiction.

# How 'Privilege' Became a Provocation

ESSAY | BY PARUL SEHGAL | JULY 14, 2015

THIS SPRING, the novelist Chimamanda Ngozi Adichie put a new spin on the commencement speech, that most staid of genres. Speaking at Wellesley College, she didn't emphasize how the graduates had been helped by their education, but how they had been hindered by it. She invoked their privilege — and her own — to describe how "privilege blinds." As a highly educated woman, she told them, she hadn't always been alert to the "nuances" of people who were different from her. "Privilege blinds, because it's in its nature to blind," she said. "Don't let it blind you too often. Sometimes you will need to push it aside in order to see clearly."

Adichie was speaking to her audience in their own language. The word "privilege" has become ubiquitous on college campuses — but in her coolness, in her ability to claim her own privilege without anxiety or abjection, she restored some dignity to an overstuffed, overheated word.

"Privilege" is as old as society itself and initially referred to wealth: "We have got to fight against privilege," George Orwell wrote. "And if the rich squeal audibly, so much the better." But when social scientists began using the word to refer to the unearned benefits afforded a group of people, the term experienced a resurgence. It has prompted flamboyant disputes on cable news, memorably between Jon Stewart and Bill O'Reilly, who debated whether privilege really exists at all. It inspires college students to fire off indignant editorials about how identity politics on campus and a culture of "checking your privilege" — examining how your perspective is shaped by your advantages — is going too far or not far enough. President Obama has been asked if he is doing enough to address white privilege in America. On the Internet, it makes for trusty kindling, and in the popular imagination, a cudgel: When people think of "privilege" being used, it's almost always as an epithet, to shame.

In the 1930s, W.E.B. Du Bois had an insight that privilege isn't only about having money — it's a state of being. He noted a "psychological wage" of whiteness: Poor whites felt that they outranked poor blacks; they could at least vote and access public schools and parks. In 1988, Peggy McIntosh, a women's studies scholar at Wellesley, expanded on the idea, publishing a list of 46 benefits of being white (for example: "I can if I wish arrange to be in the company of people of my race most of the time"; "I do not have to educate my children to be aware of systemic racism for their own daily physical protection"). "I had been taught about racism as something which puts others at a disadvantage," she wrote, "but had been taught not to see one of its corollary aspects, white privilege, which puts me at an advantage." For many, this idea of privilege was their introduction to thinking about racism not as "individual acts of meanness," in McIntosh's words, but as "invisible systems conferring unsought racial dominance." And for people of color, it was yet another powerful confirmation of their perceptions, their feeling that there were different sets of rules in place. It also made the case that failing to reckon with your privilege meant settling for a partial view of reality — Adichie's very point.

BUT THE SHINE has come off this hardy, once-helpful word. It looks a little worn, a bit blunted, as if it has been taken to too many fights. Instead of clarity, it has sown confusion: "I'm white, my husband is Latino," one woman commented on a blog post about confronting your privilege. "We have a Latino last name. Does that mean I lose some of my white privilege?" Even those who find it useful in certain contexts say the word swallows too many subtleties and individual variations. "You need to know that I was privileged," Ta-Nehisi Coates wrote on his blog for The Atlantic. "I can run you all kinds of stats on the racial wealth gap and will gladly discuss its origins. But you can't really buy two parents like I had." My own allegiance to the word is atavistic — growing up, it was one of the few words I had to understand the racism I felt so surrounded and mystified by. But now I find myself wielding the word warily, like the devalued currency it has become — dismissed as jargon or used to hector. The only reliable effect it seems to produce is panic.

In a new meme on Twitter, white men have been posting photographs of themselves lying facedown on the ground, with the hashtag #takeusdown, in mock apology for their white privilege. "I'm waiting for the Semi Truck of Social Injustice to end my privilege," one man wrote beneath a photograph of himself belly-flopped on what looked like very hot tarmac. The men appeared to be mimicking the poses of activists at "die-ins" organized to bring attention to the police killings of Michael Brown and Eric Garner. In doing so, they seemed to equate the notion of being "accused" of white privilege with being shot dead in the street. It's a comparison that would have been outrageous if it weren't so ill-conceived. If the concept of privilege was designed to enjoin people to look and listen beyond their own experience, by lying facedown on the ground, these men ensure that they see and hear nothing.

Lest it seem that outrage over being "accused" of privilege is the exclusive province of angry men on Twitter, consider Joan Didion's 2011 memoir, "Blue Nights." Didion writes about her daughter, Quintana Roo Dunne Michael, who died at 39, with a fierce tenderness. She evokes Quintana's struggles with mental illness and alcohol, as well as her enchanted childhood spent on Hollywood film sets and in the homes of movie stars, at the Dorchester, the Plaza Athénée. But when mentioning Quintana's Spanish-speaking nanny, Didion turns huffy. "'Ordinary' childhoods in Los Angeles very often involve someone speaking Spanish," she hastens to add. She wants it understood that her daughter in no way was "privileged." "'Privilege' is a judgment," she writes. "'Privilege' remains an area to which — when I think of what she endured, when I consider what came later — I will not easily cop."

The critic Maggie Nelson dissects this scene in her new book, "The Argonauts." It is strange, she writes, that Didion, who has written so brilliantly about suffering, could believe that privilege and pain are mutually exclusive. Like some of the #takeusdown demonstrators, Didion holds that hardship negates the privileges of whiteness or wealth. It's a perspective that obscures — almost willfully — what the idea of privilege was trying to illuminate in the first place: how structural privilege is, and how it manifests in the unexceptional and everyday, in what we take for granted. Think of how personal and pointed McIntosh's examples were: "I can easily buy posters, post-cards, picture books, greeting cards, dolls, toys and children's mag-azines featuring people of my race." And Nelson finds Didion's use of the word "cop" especially odd and suggestive. "The notion of privi-lege as something to which one could 'easily cop,' as in 'cop to once and be done with,' is ridiculous," she writes. "Privilege *saturates*, privilege *structures*."

"Privilege saturates" — and privilege *stains*. Which might explain why this word pricks and "opportunity" and "advantage" don't. "I can choose to not act racist, but I can't choose to not be privileged," a friend once told me with alarm. Most of us already occupy some kind of vis-ible social identity, but for those who have imagined themselves to be free agents, the notion of possessing privilege calls them back to their bodies in a way that feels new and unpleasant. It conflicts with a num-ber of cherished American ideals of self-invention and self-reliance, meritocracy and quick fixes — and lends itself to no obvious action, which is perhaps why the ritual of "confessing" to your privilege, or getting someone else to, has accumulated the meaning it has. It's the fumbling hope that acknowledging privilege could offer some tempo-rary absolution for having it.

It makes sense that we're fixated on the word "privilege" now: There has never been more ample or graphic evidence of its mate-rial and psychological benefits. Studies show that having a "black" name halves your chances of getting a job interview, and that expe-riencing racism has been linked to developing post-traumatic stress disorder, depression and breast cancer. A small University of Virginia study showed that by the age of 10, white children don't believe that black children feel the same amount of pain as they do, the first stage of dehumanization.

It's easier to find a word wanting, rather than ourselves. It's easy to point out how a word buckles and breaks; it's harder to notice how we do. "Privilege" was a ladder of a word that wanted to allow us to see a bit further, past our experiences. It's still the most powerful short-hand we have to explain the grotesque contrast between the brutal police killings of Michael Brown, Eric Garner and Tamir Rice and the treatment extended to Dylann Roof, charged with murdering nine black people last month in a church in Charleston, S.C. — captured alive, treated to a meal by the arresting officers, assigned a judge who expressed concern for his family. "Privilege" was intended to be an enticement to action, and it is still hopeful, if depleted and a little lost. It is emblematic of the kinds of pressures we put on language, our stub-born belief that the right word can be both diagnosis and cure.

# Representation and Identity in Elections

Identity politics came to the forefront of media attention during and after the U.S. presidential election of 2016. After the election, many observers noticed a deep partisan divide between the largely white supporters of President Donald Trump and minority voters, who largely favored his opponent, Hillary Clinton. Elections in 2017 and 2018 featured many diverse candidates — women, people of color and LGBTQ people — who hoped to counter what they felt was a fear of diversity sowed by President Trump and his supporters.

## Is the Slide Into Tribal Politics Inevitable?

BY BRENDAN NYHAN | NOV. 17, 2016

DONALD J. TRUMP's victory could well push the American party system toward a clash between an overwhelmingly white ethnic party and a cosmopolitan coalition of minority groups and college-educated whites.

Despite the unexpected result, Mr. Trump lost the popular vote in an election that in some respects closely resembled Barack Obama's victory over Mitt Romney in 2012 — an ordinary end to a very abnormal campaign. The power of party identification held approximately 90 percent of Republicans in Mr. Trump's camp.

However, Mr. Trump's campaign may set in motion a process that reorients American politics toward the cosmopolitanism versus nationalism divide that he emphasized, reconfiguring our party system and shaping our politics for decades to come. The power of social identity suggests that such a dynamic could be difficult to stop once set in motion.

In recent years, the Democrats and Republicans have battled along a liberal-conservative axis of conflict that emphasizes disagreement over the size and scope of government rather than divisive disputes about racial identity. During the 2008 and 2012 presidential elections, for instance, John McCain and Mr. Romney ran against Mr. Obama's domestic policy proposals on issues like health care and the economy.

After 2012, the Republican Party hoped to continue along this path and expand its appeal to young people, minorities and women. But as the political scientists Gary Miller and Norm Schofield note, candidates and parties sometimes "engage in flanking moves so as to enlist coalitions of disaffected voters." By changing positions on social issues that cut across party lines, they seek to attract voters who are only loosely attached to the other party.

Mr. Trump seems to have pulled off one of these maneuvers in shifting from traditional conservatism to a kind of race-inflected nationalism. Though the move cost him votes among college-educated whites, he attracted support among the larger group of whites without a college degree (a substantial minority of whom had backed Mr. Obama in 2012), pulling in just enough votes in the Rust Belt to tip the election.

Despite all the attention paid to economic anxiety as the basis for Mr. Trump's appeal, the evidence to date is more consistent with his brand of identity politics being the most important cause of this shift in voting patterns from 2012 (though of course economic anxiety and group animus are not mutually exclusive).

Mr. Trump's approach has the potential to transform the party system. First, the success of his campaign may encourage other Republicans to adopt his model. He has shown that the penalty for deviating from orthodox policies is minimal and that an ethno-nationalist style can have significant electoral advantages.

Second, though presidents cannot impose their will on most of domestic policy, they can help define the issues on the political agenda. In the choices that he makes, Mr. Trump may play down conflict over the size and scope of government and shift the political debate toward questions of national identity, immigration and culture.

Finally, few Republicans are likely to want to cross Mr. Trump and his energized supporters given the threat of a potential primary challenge in 2018.

Consider, for instance, Mr. Trump's decision to name as his chief strategist Steve Bannon, the head of Breitbart, a website described in an article in the conservative National Review as catering to "a small but vocal fringe of white supremacists, anti-Semites and internet trolls." Though the move lacked recent precedent, no Republicans in Congress objected, which made the issue into a partisan dispute with Democrats. Mr. Trump has also stirred emotions by promising to deport two to three million undocumented immigrants. By contrast, the fate of a tax cut — normally the top G.O.P. domestic policy priority — has received less attention (though the party will almost certainly pursue one).

Mr. Trump's success is likely to provoke a response from Democrats that could accelerate this shift. They face an outraged liberal base that is likely to reject conciliatory messages intended to win back votes among the white working class.

The party might instead double down on cosmopolitan appeals to the minority voters and college-educated white voters who were the main target of Hillary Clinton's campaign. The strategy failed in 2016, but the incentive to try again is clear. Democrats came closer to winning several Sun Belt states where minority and college-educated white populations are growing, like Arizona and Georgia, than they did in some traditional Midwest strongholds with higher numbers of noncollege whites, like Ohio and Iowa.

A focus on cosmopolitanism might make electoral sense for Democrats given the changing demographics of the country, but it could further weaken their appeal to whites without college degrees, dividing the electorate by race and class even more.

Nothing about this process is preordained, of course. Republicans may yet succeed in steering Mr. Trump toward a traditional G.O.P. agenda of tax cuts and deregulation. But the effects he could have on America's party system could be of far more lasting consequence than almost any policy he might propose.

**BRENDAN NYHAN** is a professor of government at Dartmouth College.

# White Women Voted Trump. Now What?

OPINION | BY PHOEBE LETT | NOV. 10, 2016

AROUND THE COUNTRY women weep, wondering how the glass ceiling still stands. But now is not the time to bury our faces in our hands. For white women in particular, now is the time to look in the mirror.

Ninety-four percent of black women voted for Hillary Clinton. Sixty-eight percent of Latina women did so. But 53 percent of the white female voters in this country voted for Donald Trump.

As a young white woman, I realize that white women did not do the work needed to keep Mr. Trump, and his boasts about sexual harassment, from the White House. They did not rise to the uncomfortable challenge of convincing other white women to support not just their own interests, but those of women and men of color, L.G.B.T. Americans, immigrants and people in poverty.

JEFF HALLER FOR THE NEW YORK TIMES

Trump supporters at a rally in Mobile, Ala., in August.

The problem may lie in myopia: On Tuesday, women honored suffragists by placing their "I voted" stickers on Susan B. Anthony's tombstone. How many remembered that the suffrage movement put white women first, and failed to fight for women of color?

Whatever the cause, the white women of the "pantsuit nation," as many Clinton supporters call themselves, have some work to do.

When men, awakening to the privileges their gender grants them in society, ask for a place in the feminist movement, feminists ask them to call out sexism when they see it and help other men understand what they have learned about misogyny.

It is time white women start making change within their own circles. White women must talk to their sisters, mothers, colleagues and friends about racism, homophobia, Islamophobia, transphobia and ableism. Prejudice must be called out, even in friends. These conversations may become uncomfortable, but so are these election results: 42 percent of American women voted for Trump. Ignore the calls to avoid politics at the dinner table, knowing that many Americans do not have the luxury of avoiding identity politics, because they live it every day.

We must all try to live by the words of the civil rights activist and writer Audre Lorde: "I am not free while any woman is unfree, even when her shackles are very different from my own."

**PHOEBE LETT** is an editorial assistant in The Times Opinion section.

# The Populism Perplex

OPINION | BY PAUL KRUGMAN | NOV. 25, 2016

HILLARY CLINTON WON the popular vote by more than two million, and she would probably be president-elect if the director of the F.B.I. hadn't laid such a heavy thumb on the scales, just days before the election. But it shouldn't even have been close; what put Donald Trump in striking distance was overwhelming support from whites without college degrees. So what can Democrats do to win back at least some of those voters?

Recently Bernie Sanders offered an answer: Democrats should "go beyond identity politics." What's needed, he said, are candidates who understand that working-class incomes are down, who will "stand up to Wall Street, to the insurance companies, to the drug companies, to the fossil fuel industry."

But is there any reason to believe that this would work? Let me offer some reasons for doubt.

First, a general point: Any claim that changed policy positions will win elections assumes that the public will hear about those positions. How is that supposed to happen, when most of the news media simply refuse to cover policy substance? Remember, over the course of the 2016 campaign, the three network news shows devoted a total of 35 minutes combined to policy issues — all policy issues. Meanwhile, they devoted 125 minutes to Mrs. Clinton's emails.

Beyond this, the fact is that Democrats have already been pursuing policies that are much better for the white working class than anything the other party has to offer. Yet this has brought no political reward.

Consider eastern Kentucky, a very white area which has benefited enormously from Obama-era initiatives. Take, in particular, the case of Clay County, which The Times declared a few years ago to be the hardest place in America to live. It's still very hard, but at least most of its residents now have health insurance: Independent estimates say that the uninsured rate fell from 27 percent in 2013 to 10 percent in 2016. That's the effect of the Affordable Care Act, which Mrs. Clinton promised to preserve and extend but Mr. Trump promised to kill.

Mr. Trump received 87 percent of Clay County's vote.

Now, you might say that health insurance is one thing, but what people want are good jobs. Eastern Kentucky used to be coal country, and Mr. Trump, unlike Mrs. Clinton, promised to bring the coal jobs back. (So much for the idea that Democrats need a candidate who will stand up to the fossil fuels industry.) But it's a nonsensical promise.

Where did Appalachia's coal mining jobs go? They weren't lost to unfair competition from China or Mexico. What happened instead was, first, a decades-long erosion as U.S. coal production shifted from underground mining to strip mining and mountaintop removal, which require many fewer workers: Coal employment peaked in 1979, fell rapidly during the Reagan years, and was down more than half by 2007. A further plunge came in recent years thanks to fracking. None of this is reversible.

TY WRIGHT FOR THE NEW YORK TIMES

Coal miners and their families holding campaign signs in support of Donald Trump in West Virginia, where Hillary Clinton was campaigning.

Is the case of former coal country exceptional? Not really. Unlike the decline in coal, some of the long-term decline in manufacturing employment can be attributed to rising trade deficits, but even there it's a fairly small fraction of the story. Nobody can credibly promise to bring the old jobs back; what you can promise — and Mrs. Clinton did — are things like guaranteed health care and higher minimum wages. But working-class whites overwhelmingly voted for politicians who promise to destroy those gains.

So what happened here? Part of the answer may be that Mr. Trump had no problems with telling lies about what he could accomplish. If so, there may be a backlash when the coal and manufacturing jobs don't come back, while health insurance disappears.

But maybe not. Maybe a Trump administration can keep its supporters on board, not by improving their lives, but by feeding their sense of resentment.

For let's be serious here: You can't explain the votes of places like Clay County as a response to disagreements about trade policy. The only way to make sense of what happened is to see the vote as an expression of, well, identity politics — some combination of white resentment at what voters see as favoritism toward nonwhites (even though it isn't) and anger on the part of the less educated at liberal elites whom they imagine look down on them.

To be honest, I don't fully understand this resentment. In particular, I don't know why imagined liberal disdain inspires so much more anger than the very real disdain of conservatives who see the poverty of places like eastern Kentucky as a sign of the personal and moral inadequacy of their residents.

One thing is clear, however: Democrats have to figure out why the white working class just voted overwhelmingly against its own economic interests, not pretend that a bit more populism would solve the problem.

**PAUL KRUGMAN** is an Op-Ed columnist at The New York Times.

# Why Americans Vote 'Against Their Interest': Partisanship

BY AMANDA TAUB | APRIL 12, 2017

WORKING-CLASS AMERICANS who voted for Donald J. Trump continue to approve of him as president, even though he supported a health care bill that would disproportionately hurt them.

Highly educated professionals tend to lean Democratic, even though Republican tax policies would probably leave more money in their pockets.

Why do people vote against their economic interests?

The answer, experts say, is partisanship. Party affiliation has become an all-encompassing identity that outweighs the details of specific policies.

"Partisan identification is bigger than anything the party *does*," said Frances Lee, a professor at the University of Maryland who wrote a book on partisan polarization. Rather, it stems from something much more fundamental: people's idea of who they *are*.

## PARTISANSHIP AS TRIBAL SELF-EXPRESSION

For American voters, party affiliation is a way to express a bundle of identities.

"It more or less boils down to how you see the conflicts in American society, and which groups you see as representing you," Ms. Lee said. "That often means race, and religion, and ethnicity — those are the social groups that underlie party identification."

That process is not necessarily conscious. "There's sort of an embarrassment about being a partisan," Ms. Lee said. "It's seen as admitting to a bias." That often leads people to say that they are independent, she said, but in fact most voters consistently lean toward one of the parties.

As partisanship grows, switching parties has become rare for voters. So has ticket-splitting, in which voters support different parties in presidential and down-ballot races.

But when people do switch, it is often because they feel that the other party has become a better representative of the groups that they identify with. Preliminary data suggests that is what happened with the Democratic voters who voted for Mr. Trump in 2016, said Lilliana Mason, a professor at the University of Maryland who studies partisanship.

"Older voters who scored high on racial resentment were much more likely to switch from Obama to Trump," Ms. Mason said. She believes that he successfully made a pitch to what she calls "white male identity politics," convincing older, less-educated white voters that he would represent their interests.

Economic status, it turns out, is not so important in partisanship. "Class in American politics, rich vs. poor, is just not a very good predictor of party identification," Ms. Lee said. For both rich and poor Americans, other identities take precedence.

ERIC THAYER FOR THE NEW YORK TIMES

A Trump supporter at a campaign event last June in The Woodlands, Tex.

"There are plenty of rich Democrats," Ms. Lee pointed out. "There are plenty of Republican politicians who represent poor districts."

That's not to say that the parties don't have major differences on economic matters. But, experts say, those differences matter more to elites than to rank-and-file voters.

That is why, for instance, Mr. Trump was able to win the G.O.P. nomination even though he broke with Republican ideology on economic matters like trade protectionism. His arguments played to white working-class voter identity, and that turned out to be a successful strategy even though it alienated many of the party's leaders.

But how voters choose their party is only one element of the story. The overlapping identities that underlie partisanship are also driving a form of polarization so strong that it is now essentially impossible for politicians, or the public, to avoid its influence.

## HOW IDENTITY DRIVES POLARIZATION

In 2009, when Ms. Mason was still a graduate student, she had a "eureka" moment about American politics. "I stumbled across this social psychology article from 2002 that talked about what happens when multiple identities line up together," she said in an interview. "There was all this social psychology literature about how it increases bias."

The same, she realized, was true of partisan identity. Everyone has multiple identities: racial, religious, professional, ideological and more. But while those multiple identities might once have pushed people in different partisan directions — think of the conservative Democrats of old in the South or all the liberal Republicans in the Northeast — today it's more common to line up behind one party. A white conservative who lives in a rural area and is an evangelical Christian is likely to feel that the Republican Party is the best representative of all of those separate identities, for instance. An African-American liberal who lives in a city and works in a professional job is likely to feel the same way about the Democratic Party.

Can this explain why American politics have become so polarized over the last several decades? Starting in 1980, the National Election Study, a long-running survey that tracks Americans' political preferences, showed that Republicans and Democrats were growing apart: Each reported increasingly negative opinions of the opposing party. And other data showed that polarization was seeping into nonpolitical arenas, making Republicans and Democrats less likely to marry or be friends.

Ms. Mason decided to make that the focus of her doctoral thesis, and found much to support her hypothesis: Americans' overlapping political identities were driving extreme polarization.

When multiple identities line up together, all pushing people toward the same party, partisan identity becomes a kind of umbrella for many different characteristics that people feel are important to them. That magnifies people's attachment to their team.

And that, in turn, raises the stakes of conflict with the opposing "team," Ms. Mason found. In every electoral contest or partisan disagreement, she explained, people now feel that they are fighting for many elements of who they are: their racial identity, professional identity, religious identity, even geographical identity.

"The way I think of it is, imagine that the World Series also affected the N.C.A.A. and the Super Bowl and every other team you care about," she said. "So as our identities line up with party identity, politics becomes more and more consequential."

That may have been the key to Mr. Trump's success in the 2016 election, she believes. "With Trump, if you can point to one brilliant thing he did, it's that he as a politician, kind of for the first time, said 'we're losers.' " Social psychology research has shown that the best way to get people to defend their identity is to threaten it. By saying "we don't win anymore — we're losers — and I'm going to make us win again," Ms. Mason said, Mr. Trump's pitch to voters both created the sense of threat and promised a defense: a winning political strategy for the age of identity politics.

## WANTING A PARTISAN WIN, BUT NOT A POLICY ONE

The result of those overlapping, powerful identities is that Americans have become more willing to defend their party against any perceived threat, and to demand that their politicians take uncompromisingly partisan stands.

But while those demands can affect policy, they are rooted in emotional attachments, not policy goals. "When we talk about being a sports fan, there's no policy content related to that," Ms. Mason said. "It's just this sense of connection. And that's powerful! It makes people cry. It makes people riot. There doesn't really have to be any policy content for people to get riled up, and to be extremely committed."

Ms. Mason, along with Leonie Huddy, a professor at Stony Brook University, and Lene Aaroe of Aarhus University in Denmark, conducted an experiment to test the importance of policy. They found that people responded much more strongly to threats or support to their party than to particular issues. They became angry at perceived threats to their party, and enthusiastic about its perceived successes. Their responses to policy gains and losses, by contrast, were much more muted.

That helps explain why Mr. Trump's support among Republican voters remains quite high, even though the first few months of his presidency have been plagued by scandals and political setbacks, and even though his overall national approval ratings are now very low. He has been careful to recast every potential scandal and policy struggle as a battle against the Democrats and other outside groups.

Mr. Trump has insisted, for instance, that the F.B.I. investigation into his campaign staffers' contacts with Russia is meaningless "fake news," and that the real issue is whether President Obama wiretapped him before the election. (There is no evidence thus far that any such wiretapping took place.) And when the Republican health care bill failed despite Mr. Trump's support, he at first blamed Democrats.

Republican voters may not be happy with everything the president does — many, for instance, have told reporters that they would prefer him to tweet less often, and others worry about how his health care plans will affect their families — but he is still the captain of their "team." Abandoning him would mean betraying tribal allegiance, and all of the identities that underlie it.

# The Great Political Divide Over American Identity

BY LYNN VAVRECK | AUG. 2, 2017

ARE YOU AN AMERICAN?

Chances are your answer to this question depends on whether you have (or could get) a United States passport. That is one way many people think about what it means to be American. Another way is to think less literally and more culturally. Being an American, in this sense, can conjure images of apple pie, baseball and summer picnics. It may evoke ideas about working hard and being rewarded, or treating people equally and extending everyone opportunities. We teach these notions to schoolchildren and hold them up as essentially American.

But the 2016 election made clear that there isn't universal agreement on what it means to be an American, with restrictive views centered on ethnicity and religion playing a major role in the Trump campaign. And yet trends in public opinion suggest that the nation as a whole is moving away from an exclusionary notion of American identity.

The Democracy Fund, a bipartisan foundation that funds political research, recently put a series of questions about this topic to 8,000 people who voted in the 2012 presidential election as part of its Voter Study Group collaboration. The survey was fielded in November 2016, but it included re-interviews of people who were originally surveyed in 2011, 2012 and the summer of 2016. As John Sides, a member of the consortium reported, the results reveal more consensus than you might expect about American identity, but also some stark differences across parties and even within them.

Among the questions: How important are things like speaking English or being born in the United States? Should it matter if someone has lived here only a short time or has non-European ancestors? What about religion — is being a Christian crucial?

Most Americans agree on certain things that are objectively important to calling yourself an American. Across party lines, there was strong support for the importance of respecting American political institutions and laws, having citizenship, and accepting people of diverse backgrounds. Well over half the people in both major political parties agree that these things are fundamental to being American. More than 90 percent of self-described Democrats think openness to diversity is important to American identity, and 80 percent of Republicans agree.

There was less consensus, but still strong support, for the importance of speaking English (75 percent of Democrats and 95 percent of Republicans thought this was important). Relatively few members of both parties linked American identity with being of European heritage (only 16 percent of Democrats and 23 percent of Republicans thought this was important).

Within the Republican Party, however, differences emerged with respect to the importance of European ancestry. Only 9 percent of G.O.P. primary voters who reported supporting John Kasich (when asked in a July 2016 wave of the survey) thought European background was important to being an American, while 16 percent of Ted Cruz's supporters, 22 percent of Marco Rubio's supporters and 30 percent of Mr. Trump's supporters thought so.

Across all primary candidates in both parties, Mr. Trump's backers stand out on this issue.

Between the parties, the most significant disagreements about American identity centered on the importance of living in America for most of one's life, being born in America and being a Christian. Forty-nine percent of Democrats thought it was important for people who want to call themselves American to have lived here most of their lives, and 47 percent believed being born here was important. In contrast, 63 percent of Republicans weighed spending one's life here or being born here heavily. Among those who supported Mr. Trump in primary votes, those numbers rose to 69 and 72 percent.

The role of religion in American identity revealed another divide. A third of Democrats and just more than half (56 percent) of Republicans thought being a Christian was important to being an American. Within G.O.P. primary voters, Mr. Trump's voters once again stood out. Nearly two-thirds (63 percent) of his primary supporters thought being a Christian was important to being an American.

The distinctive emphasis Mr. Trump's primary voters placed on the importance of European ancestry and Christianity explains a lot about the 2016 presidential battle over the meaning of America. Would America be "stronger together," as Hillary Clinton believed, or weaker because of the non-European, non-Christian people knocking on its door?

This context makes it easier to see why many people interpreted Mr. Trump's appeal to "make America great again" as a call to exclude some groups of people from belonging or feeling like Americans.

While Mr. Trump's focus on ethnicity, religion and American identity was the catalyst that united a relatively small set of Republican primary voters behind him and helped him defy expectations and become the G.O.P. nominee, nationwide trends in what is important to American identity have been moving in the opposite direction.

The General Social Survey asked these questions of a representative sample of Americans in surveys in 1996, 2004 and 2014. In 2004, people in America, on average, held views similar to Mr. Trump's primary voters: 64 percent of the population thought being Christian was important to being an American. This was up 10 points from the 53 percent who thought so in 1996, an increase most likely caused by the Sept. 11, 2001, terrorist attacks.

But a decade later (in 2014), the number of people who thought being Christian was important to American identity had not only gone back to where it was in 1996 but had also dropped further — nearly 10 more points — down to 44 percent on average. In the Democracy Fund study of voters in 2016, the average was 39 percent. Similarly sized drops are evident for being born in the United States and living in America for a long time.

These data clearly show that the nation as a whole is moving away from exclusionary conceptions of American identity even as Mr. Trump's strongest supporters hold on to views that look more the way the nation did in 2004 than in 2017. They found a champion among the crowded field of candidates in 2016, but it's important to keep in mind that only one of the many contenders for the Republican nomination embraced these views — even after it became clear they were popular with a key bloc of voters. The battle for the meaning of America is lopsided, and despite the recent success of exclusionary views, they are waning.

**LYNN VAVRECK**, a professor of political science at U.C.L.A., is a co-author of the coming "Identity Crisis: The 2016 Presidential Campaign and the Battle for the Meaning of America."

# A Year After Trump, Women and Minorities Give Groundbreaking Wins to Democrats

BY MICHAEL TACKETT, TRIP GABRIEL AND JOHN ELIGON | NOV. 8, 2017

IF THE 2016 presidential election reflected a primal roar from disaffected white working class voters that delivered for President Trump and Republicans, Tuesday's results showed the potential of a rising coalition of women, minorities, and gay and transgender people who are solidly aligning with Democrats.

A black transgender activist, Andrea Jenkins, was elected to the Minneapolis City Council. A Hispanic woman won the mayor's race in Topeka, Kan. A Sikh man was elected mayor in Hoboken, N.J. Latina, Vietnamese and transgender female candidates won state legislative races. Black candidates were elected lieutenant governor in New Jersey and Virginia. A Liberian refugee in Helena, Mont., was elected mayor.

Mark Keam, a Korean-American Democrat who was re-elected on Tuesday to his seat in Virginia's House of Delegates, said the wave of first-time minority candidates was a direct response to feeling snipped out of the American picture by Mr. Trump's policies and divisive language.

"In Trump's America, people are getting screwed and those getting screwed more than others are people who've never had a voice in the government," Mr. Keam said. "Those are motivations a white guy wouldn't have."

Some are skeptical of reading too much into one off-year election. And even Democrats have had heated disagreements over whether identity politics help the party or drive people away. But David Ramadan, a Republican who served in the Virginia General Assembly from 2012 to 2016 said the warning for his party was clear.

"Tuesday's results show that unless the Republicans go back to being mainstream conservatives and run on issues like education, jobs and transportations instead of sanctuary cities and Confederate statues, they will hand not only Virginia to liberals, but they will hand the country to liberals and Congress to liberals next year," Mr. Ramadan said.

## DANICA ROEM

Even before her election, Danica Roem drew national attention as a transgender woman running against a Republican who had introduced a "bathroom bill" in the Virginia Legislature to bar transgender people from restrooms.

Ms. Roem, 33, a former reporter for a newspaper in the Washington suburbs, tried to focus on issues like traffic, while fending off attacks from Republicans, including the state party, that she was morally degenerate and not really a woman.

"Help me protect conservative values in Virginia!" her opponent, Bob Marshall, a 26-year incumbent known for his social conservatism, wrote in a campaign flier.

Ms. Roem, who came out in 2013, a year after beginning her transition to a woman, campaigned in a rainbow head scarf and will be the first openly transgender person in the country seated in a state legislature.

She was born and still lives in Manassas, and is something of a policy nerd. She also sings in a heavy metal band, Cab Ride Home, which she said would be taking a hiatus while she focuses as a lawmaker on raising teacher pay, Medicaid expansion — and, a top issue in her suburban district, traffic congestion.

## JUSTIN FAIRFAX

While Ralph S. Northam earned the top headlines for his surprisingly strong win over the Republican, Ed Gillespie, the victory by Justin Fairfax in the lieutenant governor's race, also has long-term implications.

Mr. Fairfax became the second African-American to be elected to that position, which has often been a stepping stone to the governor's office, as it was for Douglas Wilder, the nation's first elected black governor, Senator Tim Kaine and Mr. Northam himself.

A former federal prosecutor and graduate of Duke University and Columbia Law School, Mr. Fairfax had never held elective office. His campaign had an upbeat feel, marked by television ads that showed him preparing peanut butter sandwiches for his young children before he drove them to school.

Mr. Fairfax will instantly be seen as a top contender for governor in Virginia in 2021. Mr. Northam is limited to one, four-year term. (Virginia governors can serve multiple terms, but not two consecutively.)

## JENNY DURKAN

Jenny Durkan, who will be Seattle's first openly lesbian mayor and its first female mayor since the 1920s is a former United States attorney and a former member of the Teamsters union.

In Seattle, where socially liberal values and a labor union history are ingrained in the political culture, Ms. Durkan bragged to voters about working as a baggage handler after college for a tiny airline in Alaska, where she was the only woman and learned how to fix a forklift. "That union job helped me pay for law school," she told voters.

Ms. Durkan, 59, calls herself a progressive Democrat who is also tough on crime. She touted her experience as the United States attorney, appointed by former President Barack Obama in 2009 — where she became a specialist in cybercrime. But taking a page from Senator Bernie Sanders, she also promised two years of free community or technical tuition to all Seattle high school graduates.

She is a daughter of political royalty in Washington, and grew up one of eight children — a big, noisy Irish Catholic family, as she has called it — led by Martin J. Durkan Sr., who served for decades in the state Legislature, and was twice a candidate for governor of Washington.

## WILMOT COLLINS

When he started reading the nasty Facebook posts and hearing the hostile comments from politicians a few years back, Wilmot Collins decided he had to do something. They were accusing refugees, like him, of being terrorists, milking the welfare system and committing crimes.

"When I started listening to the rhetoric, I said, 'This is crazy,'" said Mr. Collins, who settled in Helena, Mont., as a refugee from Liberia in 1994. "Here in Montana, we're fighting the notion that refugees are terrorists. Part of me wants to show them that, 'No, here's the face of a refugee. These are who refugees are. Here is my family. This is what refugees look like. We are not terrorists.'"

On Tuesday night, Mr. Collins's efforts came full circle when he was elected mayor of Helena, unseating the 16-year incumbent, James E. Smith. Mr. Collins is believed to be the second black person elected to serve as a mayor in Montana. Edward T. Johnson won the Helena mayoral election in 1873, according to Kate Hampton of the Montana Historical Society.

Mr. Collins, 54, said he saw his election as a repudiation of some of the restrictive immigration rhetoric of President Trump.

"It's telling the bigger America that this is not about race, this is not about national origin," Mr. Collins said. He added: "What Helena said yesterday was, 'We're looking for a good candidate and we believe in this person.'"

Mr. Collins (whose cousin, Helene Cooper, is a reporter for The New York Times) said that some of his major platform planks included providing funding for essential services like the fire and police departments, and creating more affordable housing in part because of the large populations of homeless veterans and teenagers in Helena.

Mr. Collins, who is married with two adult children, came to the United States after fleeing the civil war in Liberia. He works for the state as a child protection investigator and has been a member of the Navy Reserve for two decades.

## MICHELLE DE LA ISLA

The new mayor of Topeka, Kan., Michelle De La Isla, took a difficult and winding journey to the Midwest and politics.

Born in New York and raised in Puerto Rico, she became homeless at 17 and pregnant at 19. A pastor at the church where she sang in the choir told her she was smart and should go to college on the mainland. That led Ms. De La Isla, now 41, to Wichita State University.

Today she is a single mother of three, a son and two daughters, after escaping an abusive marriage with the help of a program at the Y.W.C.A. in Topeka, she said on Tuesday after narrowly winning the mayor's race.

"All these experiences I've turned into blessings," Ms. De La Isla said. "It's easier to serve people when you're not judging them from the get-go."

Ms. De La Isla first became involved in Topeka, a city of about 122,000 with small pockets of Hispanics and African-Americans, by counseling people about their financial credit.

That led to running Topeka Habitat for Humanity, which led to her attending City Council meetings on revitalizing the downtown. A councilman who was elected mayor suggested that she seek his seat, which she won four years ago.

"I'll never forget having a conversation with my girls: My youngest said if you get elected you're showing me I can do anything," Ms. De La Isla said. "The pressure was on. It's been a journey."

## HALA AYALA

Hala Ayala, one of two women who will be the first Latinas in the Virginia General Assembly, plunged into politics after helping to organize a contingent from Prince William County to attend the Washington Women's March in January.

"After the Women's March it was like, no more," she said. "Run for office. Make change."

Hala Ayala, third from left, is one of two Latina women in the Virginia General Assembly.

Ms. Ayala, 44, quit a job in cybersecurity for the Coast Guard to run for office. The state party emphasized that she had a security clearance to rebuff Republican TV ads and mailers raising fears of illegal immigrants and crime.

In fact, she said the attacks produced a backlash in her Northern Virginia district, which has a large military and immigrant population. Lines at polls on Tuesday were the most racially and ethnically diverse she said she had seen in a decade of volunteering.

A single mother of two adult children, aged 20 and 22, Ms. Ayala has lived in the county over 35 years. She said one voter, a father with a preschool daughter, told her he hoped she would inspire his daughter. "Maybe one day she'll run for office," he said.

# Resistance, for the Win!

OPINION  |  BY CHARLES M. BLOW  |  NOV. 9, 2017

TUESDAY NIGHT'S ELECTION RESULTS were a major shot in the arm for the anti-Donald Trump resistance and a major slap in the face for all the Democrats who caterwauled last November about how the party had focused too much on courting women and minorities, and ignored angry white men.

After Trump's election, there seemed to be a surge in coverage of these men, like The Guardian's "Trump's Angry White Men" and Time's "The Revenge of the White Man."

Mark Lilla, a professor at Columbia, lamented "identity liberalism" on the cover of The New York Times' Sunday Review, writing:

> In recent years American liberalism has slipped into a kind of moral panic about racial, gender and sexual identity that has distorted liberalism's message and prevented it from becoming a unifying force capable of governing. One of the many lessons of the recent presidential election campaign and its repugnant outcome is that the age of identity liberalism must be brought to an end.

These angry white men — who have shown little strong allegiance to liberalism — were being prioritized above people who have shown an undying devotion to liberalism: college-educated whites (particularly women), people of color and passionate progressives, which of course can be overlapping labels.

These people take identity politics to mean recognizing, listening to and trying to satisfy the particular needs of particular groups of people who have very different lived experiences in this country.

Objecting to identity politics is just a guise for objecting to politics for and about people who are not white, because as the British feminist author Laurie Penny explained to Salon in August:

> All politics are identity politics, especially the politics of the far right.

*They're about this idea of white identity, this idea of male identity that feels so under attack at the moment. When people attack identity politics, they are attacking politics that prioritizes or even includes women, people of color, queer people.*

That whole conversation about how we must reject "identity politics" left a lasting bad taste in my mouth. I will confess that I'm still smarting over the implication of those conversations, in part because as a black man in America, I have seen the corpse flower that can grow from that seed.

I am always reminded of when the Republican Party abandoned black people — who had been nothing but loyal to them — to pursue the very racists who hated black people. It was called the Southern Strategy, and it wasn't that long ago. And black people, who have never forgiven that betrayal, now vote overwhelmingly Democratic.

But the fact that Democratic strategists were even thinking of actively courting voters who turn a blind eye to — or even actively cheer — Trump's bigotry underscored for me the fact that for this party, principles can be situational.

This to me is not moderation but mollification. It is a crisis of conscience. I wrote in January that the Enlightenment must never bow to the Inquisition, and I hold fast to that position.

For me, there is no middle: If you are supporting Donald Trump, you are supporting Trumpism and all that goes with it. That means that you are supporting a modus operandi that attacks people of color on every term, but keeps white supremacists safe. You are supporting Trump's demeaning of women. You are supporting his bullying. You are supporting his corruption. You are supporting his pathological lying.

It is not the job of the resistance to drag you out of that. It is the job of the resistance only to be there when and if you tire of the darkness and crawl out into the light.

We can't warp liberalism into some sort of big-tent utopia where the lion can lie down with the lamb. We should stop trying to placate those who chafe at the very values that liberalism espouses. We don't bend; we become a beacon.

We slough off this silly, racial romance dream of chasing chimerical, oppressed, forgotten, aggrieved, angry white men. Stop trying to convince us that their American dream is now a pipe dream. Stop trying to tell us that they alone should be the focus of our pity and the subject of our weeping.

The moment you supported Trump, you forfeited access to my sympathies.

And now the resistance has flexed its muscle in Virginia and shown that the broad rainbow coalition that is America's future doesn't have to kowtow to those moaning about losing the privileges from America's past. (According to exit polls, a majority of Virginia's white voters — both men and women — still voted Tuesday for the Republican who channeled Trump's worst culture-war stances.)

Playing to the identity politics of Trump-loving angry white men — a clear expression of white supremacist patriarchy — isn't a panacea. It's not even prudent. And conversely, inclusive identity politics isn't a poison. White supremacy, and the panic induced when that supremacy is threatened, is the poison.

**CHARLES M. BLOW** is an Op-Ed columnist for The New York TImes.

# Stacey Abrams Didn't Play It Safe. Neither Do These Female Candidates.

BY SUSAN CHIRA AND MATT FLEGENHEIMER | MAY 29, 2018

THE QUESTION WENT OUT late one night on a private message chain of insurgent female candidates for Congress: Do you really attack a fellow Democrat?

"I feel like I've been pulling punches," wrote Alexandria Ocasio-Cortez, who is challenging a longtime Democratic incumbent, Joe Crowley of New York, in a primary. "Do you ever get any pushback from voters, or those who don't want 'party infighting?' "

Within the hour, peers from Texas, Washington State and North Carolina had weighed in: Keep up the fight.

"We're not trying to ask permission to get in the door," Ms. Ocasio-Cortez, a 28-year-old organizer on Bernie Sanders' presidential campaign, said in an interview.

As Democratic women run for House, Senate and state offices in historic numbers this year, many are bucking the careful and cautious ways of politics. As Stacey Abrams showed last week, a black woman can win the Democratic nomination for governor in Georgia by running a proudly liberal campaign, for instance. For dozens of these candidates, confronting President Trump and winning seats and offices for Democrats are not the only goals: They want to run and win on their own terms. Some are coming for their own party. And many are not waiting their turn, as past generations were mostly content to do.

Like Ms. Abrams, many of these challengers are women who lean left, and many are women of color, raising pointed questions for a Democratic Party wrestling with its relationship to identity politics. Some are mounting primary challenges to white male incumbents. Others are turning primaries into evermore crowded races, to the frustration of party leaders who would like to cull the fields and save resources for the general election.

Many of these contested races are pitting moderate Democrats who are aiming to woo back suburban voters and the white working class against liberals who are pursuing a turn-out-the-base strategy and are seeking to field a more diverse slate of candidates.

"I had to spend the first days of this campaign just defending my right to run," said Ayanna Pressley, the first black woman to serve on Boston's City Council, accepting a union endorsement last month in her House race against Representative Mike Capuano, a white, well-funded and consistently liberal incumbent. More than half of the district's residents are minorities, noted Ms. Pressley, who was among the first candidates last Tuesday to post congratulations to Ms. Abrams on Twitter.

"Today I stood here with people who look like my mother and represent our families and our struggle," she told the union members. "And you said, 'We choose you to lead this fight.' "

Of the 293 women who ran or are running for House and Senate as challengers so far, 54 are taking on incumbents in their own parties, according to the Center for American Women and Politics at Rutgers University. Thirty-four are in Democratic races.

The crop of renegades this year roughly falls into two categories: candidates already in public office, and newcomers who draw on some history in activism. Several of those first-time candidates are facing daunting odds because they are running in staunchly Republican districts or have little money or political networks. Past elections have generally favored candidates with traditional political experience. But then, conventional wisdom has a checkered recent track record: In that regard, Mr. Trump has shown the way.

"I feel this year we are seeing far more women who woke up one morning, turned on the TV and said, if he can be president I can run for the state legislature, Congress or governor," said Debbie Walsh, the director of the center at Rutgers. "I don't know if this will be an anomaly or this is the beginning of a shift."

For many candidates and strategists, the oft-invoked analogy for the 2018 campaigns is 1992, when women swept into office in part on a tide of outrage about the grilling of Anita Hill by an all-male, all-white Senate Judiciary Committee during the Clarence Thomas hearings.

Marsha Blackburn first ran for Congress in 1992, when she was a Tennessee businesswoman and local Republican county chair. She had an anti-regulation, lower taxes message, but ended up losing to the Democratic incumbent. She was undeterred. Drawing on the skills and connections she forged, she went on to win a seat first in the State Legislature and then, by 2002, in Congress. "You begin to build that network," she said. "Then you use that network."

She is now running for the Senate seat vacated by Bob Corker, in a tough race against Phil Bredesen, the former Democratic governor. Tennessee, she points out, has never elected a woman senator or governor.

Several candidates this year say they will not measure success solely on whether they win in the end.

Linsey Fagan, 32, a former Sanders delegate running for the first time in Texas, said she hoped to tilt the debate leftward and lay the groundwork for future runs if she does not prevail in the fall. Ms. Fagan has already won her primary and will face Representative Michael Burgess in November in a heavily Republican district around Dallas.

"We've just learned everything from scratch together," she said of fellow first-time candidates around the country, with whom she has formed relationships. "If I can inspire more people to run fearlessly and in a way that's authentic, that would be a positive outcome for me."

Democratic challengers in such deep-red territory have expressed frustration at times with a national party that seems disinclined to help them face down the long odds, as party officials expect little return for any investment.

But there have been success stories. In Kentucky last week, Amy McGrath, a former Marine fighter pilot, defeated Jim Gray, a well-liked mayor of Lexington, in a Democratic primary, thrilling even many in the party who had initially preferred Mr. Gray in a district that the Republican incumbent won by 22 points last time.

In other areas, women candidates have run into more significant obstacles created by the Democratic Congressional Campaign Committee, the campaign arm for House Democrats. In February, the group posted negative research to undercut a liberal insurgent, Laura Moser, in a Houston-area primary, stirring progressive outrage. Despite those efforts, Ms. Moser qualified for the runoff election against Lizzie Pannill Fletcher, a lawyer; Ms. Fletcher prevailed last week.

In Orange County, Calif., the committee has taken a side against Mai Khanh Tran, a Vietnamese-born pediatrician whose biography has attracted wide attention. It endorsed Gil Cisneros, a Navy veteran and former Republican whom the group believes has a better chance in November.

Then there is the Wisconsin district being vacated by House Speaker Paul Ryan. National Democrats, including the campaign committee, donors and several left-leaning organizations, have rallied behind Randy Bryce, a mustachioed ironworker with a popular Twitter account, @IronStache, and well-stocked campaign coffers. His primary opponent, Cathy Myers — a school board member and longtime teacher — has not appreciated the perceived coronation.

"They thought they should match Trump's testosterone with more testosterone," she said of her skeptics in an interview. "I've been told by some people, mostly his supporters, that I should just step aside, that it's his turn. I really think that's a bad way to choose a representative."

Brianna Wu represents another dynamic this year: a political novice confronting a longstanding but more conservative Democratic incumbent, in this case Stephen Lynch of Massachusetts.

As one of the several female video game developers who were targets of death threats in the outpouring of vitriol known as Gamergate, Ms. Wu has a national profile, a motorcycle and a Porsche in her driveway, and gulps Soylent, the tech drink of choice, for lunch. But her long-shot bid has quickly run up against institutional barriers.

She is new to her district; her opponent is well-funded; and her upstart candidacy faces open antagonism. Trying to draw up a plan to address a water crisis in the town of Hingham, she said she reached out to a local official and a federal environmental employee who told her they were friends of Mr. Lynch's and declined to help.

"The doors slam shut," she said. "I feel like I'm running more against the Democratic Party in my state than against Stephen Lynch at times."

Even if she fails, she says, she will try again in 2020.

Ms. Pressley, running in the congressional district next door, is seen as a more potent threat for an upset.

Her decision to run shocked Boston's political establishment, and even John Lewis, the civil rights icon, endorsed Mr. Capuano, as did the political arm of the Congressional Black Caucus. Although Ms. Pressley was hailed as a rising political star by Emily's List in 2015, the organization has not endorsed either candidate in the primary. Undeterred, Ms. Pressley is laying down a stark generational, gender and racial challenge.

"It's her time," said Gene Van Buren, a shop steward at Harvard Law School for Local 26, the hotel and food service union that endorsed her. "She doesn't have to wait her turn."

To those who say there is little policy daylight between Ms. Pressley and her opponent, Mr. Capuano — who is well-funded and generally well-regarded by progressives — she argues that her life story allows her to design policies that better serve her constituents. Speaking after her union endorsement, Ms. Pressley recounted a father battling addiction, a single mother working multiple jobs, and surviving childhood sexual abuse and campus sexual assault. She emphasized that she has a track record of earning votes from white neighborhoods as well as minority ones.

While she parsed her words carefully, the implications were clear: in solidly Democratic Massachusetts, longtime incumbents will prevail, foreclosing opportunities for younger, more diverse candidates to run. Seven of the state's nine congressional districts are represented by white men; two are white women.

"This district is not in danger of being represented by a Republican," Ms. Pressley said. "If this were an open seat, you would have six, eight, maybe 12 people running. They would all be Democratic and they would all vote the same way. And you would not be saying, 'Oh, y'all need to get out except for one person.' "

# 'Don't Run This Year': The Perils for Republican Women Facing a Flood of Resistance

BY KATE ZERNIKE | AUG. 13, 2018

The energy in the midterms is working against female Republican candidates, who are reluctant or unable to claim any advantage to being a woman among voters.

SAN JUAN CAPISTRANO, CALIF. — Diane Harkey, the Republican candidate for California's 49th Congressional District, recognizes that President Trump "doesn't make women real comfortable."

Men just have a different style, she said: "They're more warrior-oriented. We are a little more consensus-builders."

But she laughs off the idea of campaigning as a woman. "I want all voters, I like men too," she said. "I don't think it helps to talk about gender."

It may be the year of the woman in midterm campaigns across the country, but Ms. Harkey is not embracing it here in one of the nation's most hotly contested congressional elections. The passion is far more evident 30 miles south of here, in the offices of a new group called Flip the 49th, whose weekly protests following Mr. Trump's inauguration drove the Republican incumbent, Darrell Issa, from his seat. Now, it is working feverishly to elect the male Democrat running against Ms. Harkey.

"She's anti-health care, anti-gun control, anti-family, anti-immigrant, anti-environment," said Mary Schrader, a Flip volunteer who was a Republican until 2016. "She's completely out of touch with the women in her district."

This is the bind for Republican women running for office in the Trump era. The energy among women that started with the marches after the president's inauguration is against them — surveys have shown that 70 percent of the membership of local resistance groups, and almost all the top leadership, are women. And having long resisted identity politics, Republican women are reluctant or unable to claim any advantage to being a woman among voters.

Republican women running in swing districts are instead left to carefully carve out the separation between themselves and Mr. Trump, a president who was elected with the biggest gender gap ever recorded, and who regularly dismisses female officeholders as "crazy" and "low I.Q."

Those running in districts where the president is popular have been punished for so much as criticizing him for incivility.

"We've told a lot of women, 'Don't run this year,'" said Meghan Milloy, the co-founder of Republican Women for Progress, which helps to promote moderate female Republicans. "We've told them, 'You're a great candidate, if it were any other year you would win.' We don't want these women, who have such potential, to lose and get down and get out of politics."

There is a record number of Democratic women running for the House this year, but Republican women did not break the record they set in 2010 — when the "resistance" energy was on the right. Only about 14 percent of Republican House candidates are women, compared with about a third of Democratic candidates, according to the Center for American Women and Politics at Rutgers.

Representative Elise Stefanik, a New York Republican who is leading her party's recruitment efforts in the House, credits several candidates with keeping the party competitive in districts where Hillary Clinton won in 2016 — Young Kim in Southern California, for example, and Lea Marquez Peterson in Arizona.

Ms. Stefanik argued that Republican women connect better to voters. "Democratic women are running in response to the Trump administration," she said. "With my candidates I've worked to recruit, it's more about representing their communities and their districts."

In states and districts, though, the party has been slower to support Republican women.

Carla Nelson, running for an open House seat in southern Minnesota, has the endorsement of four national conservative women's groups, nine incumbent congresswomen and the National Rifle Association. She beat an incumbent Democrat to win her current seat in the State Senate.

But in the primary on Tuesday, local party organizations are supporting Jim Hagedorn, who has run for the seat and lost three times, even in 2016 when Mr. Trump won the district by 15 points.

"Locally it's different," Ms. Nelson said. "All the good ol' boys begged me not to run."

Mr. Hagedorn has a trail of blog posts derogating women. He described the nomination of Harriet Miers in 2005 as an attempt "to fill the bra of Supreme Court Justice Sandra Day O'Connor" and in 2008, he thanked John McCain "on behalf of all red-blooded American men" for his vice-presidential pick — "SARAH'S HOT!" he wrote — leading a columnist for the conservative Washington Examiner to label him in April "the worst midterm candidate in America."

"The mailers would write themselves," Ms. Nelson said. It was no wonder, she added, that the Republican Party is "struggling to earn the support of women in the voting booth."

Republican voters may be less inclined to support women: 13 percent of Republican primary winners so far are women, compared with 42 percent among Democrats, according to the Rutgers center.

Ms. Nelson sounds like many Democratic women when she describes why she is running in a year when the odds are so against her.

"The need is so great for someone like me who has a track record of getting things done," she said. "I just can't sit on the sidelines."

Jenifer Sarver, who ran unsuccessfully in a crowded primary in Texas's solidly red 21st District, echoed that reasoning. But while Ms. Nelson largely aligns with the president, Ms. Sarver, a former aide to Sen. Kay Bailey Hutchison, had written about her decision to vote for Mrs. Clinton over Mr. Trump in 2016.

"I sat back and said, 'Do I want to be somebody on the sidelines throwing rocks or do I want to jump in and make a difference?' " she said. "My message was, 'I want to stand next to him when he's delivering conservative policies I agree with but be the first person to call out the incivility I see.' "

She was "blown away," she said, by the support from many voters. One man, she said, told her, "My New Year's resolution was to only vote for female candidates."

But others told her that they could never vote for her because of her vote for Mrs. Clinton, and her primary opponents pounced on her for saying the Republican Party did not do a good enough job representing women and young people. Consultants told her to "run to the right and equivocate later."

"That's what people are disgusted with in politics," said Ms. Sarver, who came in fifth out of 18 candidates in the March primary. "I would rather lose with grace than lie to voters."

"Republican women have always said we don't play identity politics," she said. "How we address that going forward is a really big problem."

But the biggest problem for Republican women this year is what Ms. Harkey told the crowd of 80 people who gathered to open her headquarters on a steamy August Saturday. "The energy is on the other side," she said.

"Republicans are going, 'Are you Trump or are you not Trump?' 'Are you this or are you that?' " she said. "You know what? This is no time to worry. Just get out and vote, and vote for the party, people, because the other side has gone way far left and it's going to continue."

The district of red-roofed Spanish-style McMansions and oceanside golf courses stretches from southern Orange County to northern San Diego County and includes the Marine base at Camp Pendleton. The crowd cheering Ms. Harkey included several veterans and a woman with a sparkling flag pin. A leader of a local Republican women's club noted proudly that her red dress was from Ivanka Trump's label.

As Ms. Harkey called out to make sure she had not missed any local officials — "School board, water board, anything else?" — a man in the crowd replied, "I'm all for waterboarding!"

Ms. Harkey told her story of arriving in California as a young girl from Illinois and having to peel onions with the Mexican bracero workers to earn $11 for her first Barbie doll. She went to community college and the University of California-Irvine, working her way up in banking to become mayor of Dana Point, a wealthy oceanfront enclave. She served six years in the California State Assembly and is now a member of a board that reviews state tax assessments.

After nearly two decades of voting Republican in presidential races, the district went for Mrs. Clinton by 7 points in 2016. And Pat Bates, a state senator, warned the crowd at Ms. Harkey's headquarters that Democrats had "overperformed" in their voter registration efforts in the June primaries.

"We need boots on the ground," she said. "Every single Republican has got to vote or we're looking at a socialist southern Orange County and north San Diego, I kid you not."

The women at the Flip the 49th headquarters, who worked hard for that overperformance, began their activism out of concerns about the Trump administration dismantling the Affordable Care Act. They held weekly protests outside the office of Mr. Issa, a leading tormentor of Barack Obama and Mrs. Clinton, and once brought a cake in the shape of a Hawaiian shirt to encourage him to retire early; they returned to celebrate the next day when he announced he would.

They began calling themselves ReSistas, and by November had joined up with Flip the 49th to rent office space in Carlsbad. A Trump effigy stands in one corner and across the window is a banner reading "We the People" embroidered by Karin Brennan, a former Sergeant in Army intelligence who joined the group.

About 200 people showed up — and stayed — for a six-hour training session on how to canvass voters.

In the primaries in June, the group reached 57,000 voters by phone or door-knocks, turning out more Democrats than Republicans in a district that is known as the birthplace of the modern right.

"Eighteen months ago if you asked me my congressional district, I would have said I have to look it up on Google," said one volunteer, Ellen Montanari.

With so many women running this year, the women here wanted to support a female candidate. But they believe Mike Levin, the Democratic opponent, will support what they see as women's issues, particularly health care and gun control.

"You can have a female candidate," said Terra Lawson-Remer, a founder of Flip the 49th. "But you need an army to take power."

Ms. Harkey was endorsed by Mr. Issa. "They're trying to bank on the R next to her name," said Nikki Faddick, a co-leader for a local chapter of Moms Demand Action, a gun control group.

But Ms. Harkey, while a loyal Republican, is aware that she needs to choose her words carefully. "I would like to see the president tweet less and govern a little more," she said in an interview.

The crowd at her headquarters seemed mostly concerned about illegal immigrants taking advantage of the system. Ms. Harkey returned to her story about the braceros, noting that Mexican workers can come across the border on day passes to work in California's agricultural industry. Her voice betrayed a tinge of exasperation.

"If the president wants his wall, he needs his wall," Ms. Harkey told them. "Just do it, you know? It's not that big a deal."

# CHAPTER 3

# Race and Representation in Media

Backlash against identity politics can, in its most extreme form, lead to racism. But identity politics can also make nonwhite Americans and other disadvantaged groups feel more included in the political process and beyond. Advocates for more diverse representation argue that, for blacks, Latinos, Native Americans, Asian-Americans and other minorities, seeing people who share their identity represented in films, books and other media helps to build a more inclusive society for all.

## The Real 'Trump Effect' for Young Latinos

OPINION | BY ROBERTO SURO | MAY 27, 2016

DURING A SWING through California earlier this month, Hillary Clinton tried to celebrate Cinco de Mayo with a rally in East Los Angeles, the Mexican-American heartland where she won overwhelming support from Latinos of all ages in the 2008 primary. But this year, everything is different. Hecklers interrupted her repeatedly, and on the street her supporters faced taunts from a gantlet of demonstrators blaming her for President Obama's deportation of some Central American asylum seekers.

The disaffection and distrust evident in so much of the American electorate festers with special ferocity among young Latinos, the fastest growing segment of the American electorate. Looking at them we can see what this campaign is doing to all of us.

The laws of physics, if not elections, suggest that the Republican Party's embrace of white identity politics will provoke an equal and opposite reaction among nonwhites. But don't look for young Latinos to adopt traditional minority group politics as practiced by the Democratic officeholders, the corporate diversity officers and advocacy groups that constitute the Latino establishment. We all know by now that 2016 is a bad year for establishments.

Millennials, measured as adults born after 1981, make up 44 percent of the Latino electorate, a far greater share of eligible voters than among any other racial or ethnic group. Every year 800,000 native-born Latinos reach voting age. About half of those voters are the children of immigrants — they're animated by Donald J. Trump's bullying and some are fighting back, as they have at some Trump rallies.

Democratic primary exit polls show that Mrs. Clinton has won Latino voters over Senator Bernie Sanders by roughly two-to-one so far. In California, however, surveys show a tightening race in the June 7 primary. A close look at the data reveals a generational divide. Young Latinos are strongly supporting Mr. Sanders, while their parents' generation backs Mrs. Clinton.

Latinos have a poor record of voter turnout, and young Latinos are the worst among them. But regardless of their effect on Mrs. Clinton's immediate prospects, Latino millennials will change the ways we think about identity politics. They may finally explode the myth of a monolithic Latino vote. They are pressing policy demands, not easily satisfied with token appointments and the other palliatives offered to minority groups.

"El viejito," the affectionate term for an old man being applied to the Vermont senator, appears to have energized young Latinos with his demonization of corporations, banks and the politicians he casts as their servants, according to the polls. His impact could manifest in the ways young Latinos approach immigration.

For more than three decades, efforts to overhaul the immigration system have followed a "grand bargain" approach. Until Mitt Romney broke the pattern in 2012, presidential candidates of both parties endorsed a reform strategy that offered some kind of legalization for unauthorized immigrants in exchange for giving employers access to foreign workers through legal channels. Enforcement would increase along the way.

The grand bargain has been trashed in this year's campaign. The two most prominent Republican proponents, Jeb Bush and Marco Rubio, didn't make it past March. And, although he supports comprehensive immigration reform, Mr. Sanders relentlessly attacks the kind of deal-making between business and government that a bargain represents.

A nationwide survey by Latino Decisions, a firm that works for the Clinton campaign, shows that young Latinos by margins of two-to-one compared with older Latinos find Mr. Sanders more pro-immigrant than Mrs. Clinton and that they are more likely to vote for him because of his immigration stands.

After flocking to Mr. Sanders, young Latinos should be less likely than ever to support a future deal that trades legalization for worker visas. Many have already rejected a view of immigrants as an economic commodity, a labor input, to be bartered. Rather than responding to Mr. Trump's tribalism with tribalism of their own, they are invoking foundational truths.

The new approach was born during President Obama's first term with campaigns on behalf of the Dreamers, unauthorized migrants brought here as children who are now in college or the military. Seeking legal status, they present themselves as "Americans in all but name," as people meeting society's expectations by studying and serving. They provided the impetus behind Mr. Obama's executive orders, now tied up in a Supreme Court case, which would give some parents of United States citizens temporary reprieve from deportation.

When they demonstrate wearing caps and gowns and carrying American flags, Dreamers are proud Latinos, but that is not the basis of their demands. They are pledging allegiance to a traditional form of American civic engagement because they believe they have earned the privilege.

The number of legal immigrants becoming United States citizens has surged since the campaign got underway, and although the data is still preliminary, some advocates see a "Trump effect" at work. This suggests that broad segments of Latinos have responded to the Republican nominee's embrace of white identity by embracing a version of American identity that is not based on ethnicity but on principles.

Last week, Jeh Johnson, the secretary of Homeland Security, was faced with hecklers as he delivered a commencement address at Georgetown University. The "UndocuHoyas" protested deportation orders against Central Americans who had been denied asylum in rushed hearings with no chance for legal counsel. Mr. Johnson acknowledged the protests graciously, saying, "in this free country, you have an important role, your views matter."

These protests are not about language, nationality, skin color or any other kind of group identity. Instead, the fight is over the universal right of the individual to have claims fairly adjudicated by the state.

Young Latinos are responding to Mr. Trump's vision of Americans as a people of kindred blood with a vision of the United States as a place of kindred spirits. Those young Latinos are putting forward a message that might help us out of the mess we've made this year. If they turn out at the same rate as white millennials, they would bring an estimated more than a million new voters to the polls and might affect the results as well.

**ROBERTO SURO** is a professor of public policy and journalism at the University of Southern California.

# Identity Politics and a Dad's Loss

OPINION | BY NICHOLAS KRISTOF | DEC. 8, 2016

THIS FALL I SAT DOWN in Tulsa, Okla., with a black pastor whose unarmed son, Terence Crutcher, had been shot dead on the street by a white police officer.

The Rev. Joey Crutcher told me that Terence's killing was just the latest loss his family had suffered. He had also lost a child to crib death years ago, and another to cancer. In addition, his grandson had been shot dead while driving home from church in a gang hit that was a case of mistaken identity.

Such heartbreak: Three children and a grandchild dead, each for a different reason. I've been thinking of the Crutchers because of the debate raging in the Democratic Party about its future. One faction argues that the left became too focused on "identity politics," fighting

ANDREA MORALES FOR THE NEW YORK TIMES

The Rev. Joey Crutcher has suffered many family tragedies.

for the rights of Muslims, gays, blacks and Latinos but neglecting themes of economic justice that would appeal to everyone, working-class whites in particular.

Mark Lilla of Columbia University helped spark the civil war with a provocative essay in The Times warning that "American liberalism has slipped into a kind of moral panic about racial, gender and sexual identity that has distorted liberalism's message and prevented it from becoming a unifying force."

Speaking in Boston, Senator Bernie Sanders partly endorsed Lilla's principle: "One of the struggles that you're going to be seeing in the Democratic Party is whether we go beyond identity politics. I think it's a step forward in America if you have an African-American C.E.O. of some major corporation. But you know what, if that guy is going to be shipping jobs out of this country, and exploiting his workers, it doesn't mean a whole hell of a lot whether he's black or white or Latino."

ANDREA MORALES FOR THE NEW YORK TIMES

A memorial to Terence Crutcher, near the spot where he was shot and killed in an encounter with the Tulsa police.

Lilla and Sanders have a legitimate point, and it's clear in retrospect that the Democrats should have talked more about jobs and fairness for all. But Lilla and Sanders's argument also collides with the basic truth that it's not possible to have a serious conversation about justice, jobs and opportunity in America without talking frankly about race, gender and ethnicity.

Consider the Crutcher family: Each of the children's deaths wasn't exactly about race, yet each was linked to it. Young black men are disproportionately likely to be stopped by police officers, and shot dead by them. Crib death and cancer both are more lethal among African-Americans, because of disparities in incomes and health care. And crime in America disproportionately involves blacks, as both victims and arrested perpetrators.

So, sure, Democrats sometimes go overboard with identity and can do a far better job appealing to ALL who have been left behind — but identity still matters profoundly. The Crutchers have lost four young people, each in a way that statistically suggests a racial element.

How can we discuss a way forward without acknowledging that race is an issue here?

The blunt truth is that America's most egregious failures have often involved identity, from slavery to anti-Catholic riots, from the Chinese Exclusion Act to the internment of Japanese-Americans, from unequal pay to acquiescence in domestic violence and sex trafficking. Ditto for the threats by President-Elect Donald Trump to deport 11 million immigrants or to register Muslims.

Yet Lilla and Sanders are right that identity sometimes has distracted from the distress in working-class white America. Life expectancy for blacks, Latinos and other groups has been increasing; for middle-aged whites, it has been dropping. Likewise, the race gap in education used to be greater than the "class gap"; now the class gap is greater.

It's also true that broad efforts to create opportunity would help not only working-class whites, but also working-class blacks, Latinos and others.

I once asked Bryan Stevenson, the civil rights lawyer, how to think of the class gap versus the race gap, and he joked that for the many people caught in the criminal justice system who are both poor and black, "it's like having two kinds of cancer at the same time."

So do we really need to choose between identity and justice? Can't we treat both cancers?

In moving beyond that dichotomy, maybe we can find some inspiration from Reverend Crutcher, who is truly something of a saint: He told me that he forgives the white officer who shot his son and prays for her.

"Every night, my wife and I cry because we see our son with his hands up," he said. But he added, speaking of the officer who shot him: "She's got people around her who are hurting, too. My heart goes out to her."

Crutcher is modeling the broadest possible inclusiveness. Yes, there's a tension between focusing on bigotry and highlighting jobs. Yes, Democrats should more clearly emphasize economic justice for all, including struggling whites. But I hope that Democrats won't needlessly squabble over whether to prioritize identity or justice.

Like Reverend Crutcher, we can reach for both.

**NICHOLAS KRISTOF** is an Op-Ed columnist for The New York Times.

# What Donald Trump Doesn't Know About Black People

OPINION | BY MICHAEL ERIC DYSON | DEC. 17, 2016

IN 2005, after Hurricane Katrina, Kanye West appeared on live TV during a celebrity fund-raiser for victims of the disaster and said, "George Bush doesn't care about black people." This wasn't based on intimate knowledge of Mr. Bush's racial views, but rather on his treatment of black people in a time of crisis.

Donald J. Trump, who met with Mr. West this past week to discuss "multicultural issues," according to the rapper, hasn't been in charge yet to steer black Americans through a crisis. But we have seen enough of his views and behaviors to hazard a guess at how he thinks.

It may be that Mr. Trump's views reveal something just as devastating as not caring for black people: not knowing us.

Mr. Trump is not alone in this deliberate ignorance, as postelection calls on the left to forget about identity politics have shown. If there is a dirty secret in American life, it is this: The real unifying force in our national cultural and political life, beyond skirmishes over ideology, is white identity masked as universal, neutral and, therefore, quintessentially American. The greatest purveyors of identity politics today, and for the bulk of our country's history, have been white citizens.

There is a cost to ignorance and the hate that can grow from it. In his eulogy for the Rev. Clementa Pinckney, who was killed in 2015 by Dylann S. Roof, President Obama spoke of the proud history of Reverend Pinckney's church and community. He noted that we couldn't know what the killer understood of the community or the lives he was taking, but he did know hate. Mr. Roof was found guilty of that Charleston massacre on Thursday, his violent acts a reminder — not one we needed — of the price ignorance and hate can exact.

Donald J. Trump attended a service at the Great Faith Ministries International church in Detroit in September.

"I would be a president for all of the people, African-Americans, the inner cities," President-elect Trump declared during the second presidential debate. "Devastating what's happening to our inner cities," he lamented. "You go into the inner cities and — you see it's 45 percent poverty. African-Americans now 45 percent poverty in the inner cities."

Mr. Trump's views on black people, poverty and cities were quickly challenged as myopic and ill informed. But the administration he is building is emblematic of his ignorance.

The only African-American member of his designated cabinet is Ben Carson, who was tapped for Housing and Urban Development. Mr. Carson was a beloved American icon, a man who endured a hard-scrabble childhood in Detroit to become a famous physician. But his turn to right-wing petulance, with a bow to kooky comparisons of Obamacare to slavery, considerably soiled his reputation. If his story was once emblematic of beating the odds to become a success, he is now a different kind of symbol — of how little Mr. Trump knows, or cares, about African-Americans.

Similarly, his pick of Senator Jeff Sessions as his attorney general — a man who according to testimony before Congress once joked that the only problem with the K.K.K. was the group's drug use, deemed a white lawyer with black clients a race traitor and dismissed civil rights groups as "un-American" — proves Mr. Trump cares little for the interests of the African-American citizens he will serve in the Oval Office.

During his presidential campaign Mr. Trump tweeted out a grossly inaccurate image from a nonexistent "Crime Statistics Bureau" that suggested that the bulk of white people are killed by black people — a belief that white bigots have long parroted as the reason for their racist revenge.

Mr. Trump argued that "African-American communities are absolutely in the worst shape they've ever been in before. Ever, ever, ever." President Obama drolly declared, "I mean, he missed that whole civics lesson about slavery or Jim Crow."

Mr. Obama's retort underscores a troubling truth: Mr. Trump's vast ignorance of black life leads him to exaggerate the perils confronting black Americans in all the wrong ways. He overlooks the nation's vicious history of racism to proclaim that this is the worst racial epoch ever. It is a convenient ruse to make the period under President Obama a foil to his heroic rescue of black people through his magical political powers.

The road ahead is not easy, primarily because Mr. Trump's ignorance about race, his critical lack of nuance and learning about it, exists among liberals and the white left, too.

From the start of his 2016 presidential campaign, Bernie Sanders was prickly about race, uncomfortable with an outspoken, demanding blackness, resistant to letting go of his preference for discussing class over race. He made efforts to improve the way he spoke about the realities of racial discrimination. But Mr. Sanders seemed to remain at heart a man of the people, especially if those people were the white working class.

Since the election, Mr. Sanders has sounded an increasingly familiar theme among liberals that they should "go beyond identity politics." He warned that "to think of diversity purely in racial and gender terms is not sufficient," and that we need candidates "to be fighters for the working class and stand up to the corporate powers who have so much power over our economic lives."

In a recent speech in California, Mr. Sanders said that it is "very easy for many Americans to say, I hate racism, I hate homophobia, I hate sexism," but that "it is a little bit harder for people in the middle or upper middle class to say, maybe we do have to deal with the greed of Wall Street."

This is a nifty bit of historical revisionism. For the longest time there was little consideration for diversity, even among liberal elites, much less the white middle and working classes. It seems more than a little reactionary to blame the loss of the election on a brand of identity politics that even liberals were slow to embrace.

Attention to diversity and identity does not undercut our nation's embrace of democratic ideals; it strengthens them. The black struggle for freedom has ensured that other groups could follow along in the wake of our demand for equality. When the 1964 civil rights bill was in doubt in Congress, white opponents of the bill thought they could sink it by attaching the issue of gender, hoping to appeal to the sexism of those who might otherwise be cajoled to offer their support. Instead, the bill passed, and paved the way for both black rights and those of women. What's good for black people is good for the nation.

When it comes to the white working class, however, that is almost impossible to see.

The interests of the white working class have often been used by white political elites to stave off challenges to inequality and discrimination by black folk and other minority groups.

In the middle of the 20th century, labor unions curtailed opportunity for black workers by protecting the race-based interests of the white working and middle class. In the late 1960s, Richard M. Nixon even supported a version of affirmative action because he deemed it useful to break unions by accusing them of racial exclusion. In the 1980s, Ronald Reagan appealed to disaffected white Democrats who resented being forced to share a small measure of the gains they had accumulated through bigotry and often official discrimination.

Now we hear again the cry that the neglected white working class is the future of American progressive politics. The tragedy is that much of the professed concern about the white working class is a cover for the interests of white elites who evoke working-class solidarity to combat racial, sexual and gender progress.

Identity has always been at the heart of American culture. We must confront a truth that we have assiduously avoided: The most protected, cherished and nurtured identity of all has been white identity. After all, the needs of the black and brown working classes, which are not exclusively urban, are, again, even in progressive quarters, all but forgotten.

Mr. Trump, and to a degree, the liberals and progressives who advocate a vision of America that spurns identity politics, make one thing clear: The real unifying force in American political life is whiteness, no matter its party, gender, region or, at times, even its class.

MICHAEL ERIC DYSON, a professor of sociology at Georgetown, is the author of the forthcoming "Tears We Cannot Stop: A Sermon to White America" and a contributing opinion writer.

# Is All This Talk of Racism Bad for Democrats?

OPINION | BY DAVID LEONHARDT | JAN. 16, 2018

"I WANT THEM to talk about racism every day," Steve Bannon said last summer. "If the left is focused on race and identity, and we go with economic nationalism, we can crush the Democrats."

He's not completely wrong. When white working-class voters focus on the white part of their identity, Republicans benefit. When they focus on the working-class part, Democrats benefit. (Ezra Klein reviews the evidence here.) And whether you like it or not, white working-class voters are extremely important to determining control of state governments, Congress and the White House.

So are progressives making a mistake by spending so much time in recent days talking about President Trump being a racist? No — with a big caveat.

It is not a mistake for substantive reasons: History shows that racism becomes even more dangerous when it's allowed to go unchecked. And it's not a mistake for political reasons too: There are a significant number of independents and Republicans, including minorities and suburban college graduates, who are turned off by Trump's race-baiting.

But it's also important to distinguish between the current moment and the remainder of 2018. Calling out Trump as a racist is the right thing to do in the days immediately following comments like his vulgar denigration of Haitians and others last week. It should not become the centerpiece of the Democrats' 2018 strategy.

That centerpiece needs to be a principled populism that causes voters — white, black, Latino and Asian — to think about their economic interests. Trump certainly can be a huge part of the strategy. The president is almost always the central issue in a midterm election. The key is how Democrats talk about him.

Emphasizing the ways he's hurting the middle class and working class has almost no downside. It turns off no substantial group of voters. It can win over swing voters and motivate reliably progressive ones.

Race is different. When it's at the center of the political debate, a large group of voters can become more likely to choose white-nationalist candidates like Trump, as Bannon understood — and exploited — in 2016.

You can lament that fact. I certainly do. But don't make the mistake of denying it.

**DAVID LEONHARDT** is an Op-Ed columnist at The New York Times.

# We Got Rid of Some Bad Men. Now Let's Get Rid of Bad Movies.

OPINION | BY LINDY WEST | MARCH 3, 2018

THE OSCARS ARE HERE: the first Oscars since powerful men started falling to #MeToo, a Trump-era Oscars, a #TimesUp Oscars, an Oscars in the shadow of "Black Panther." Some big chairs will be empty. Some big secrets will stalk the red carpet, newly unleashed.

In an America where the ruling party seems willing to sacrifice many things — including decency and justice — to reassert white Christian masculinity as the tentpole of the universe, the best picture category offers a contrasting vision: a flaw-free indictment of that same colonial pathology ("Get Out"), a blazing affirmation of young womanhood ("Lady Bird") and an aching gay romance ("Call Me by Your Name"), among others.

Jordan Peele has the chance to become the first black person ever to win best director; Greta Gerwig would be only the second woman. Yance Ford, whose film "Strong Island" is up for best documentary feature, would be the first trans director to win an Oscar. Vulture reported last week that some older Academy voters refused to even watch "Get Out," calling it "not an Oscar film," a dismissal more air horn than dog whistle. Identity politics loom large over the 90th Academy Awards, as well they should.

TV and film are in the thick of an unprecedented sociopolitical reckoning, the first ever of such scale and ferocity, a microcosm of our ever-more-literal national culture war. But to make that reckoning stick, we have to look ahead and ask ourselves what we want of this new Hollywood, and look back to avoid repeating the past.

Hollywood is both a perfect and bizarre vanguard in the war for cultural change. Perfect because its reach is so vast, its influence so potent; bizarre because television and movies are how a great many toxic ideas embedded themselves inside of us in the first place.

When I was growing up, I didn't chafe at the shallow, exploitative representations of my gender that I saw on screen; I took notes. I added item after item to my mental lists of how to be a woman and the things I should yearn for and tolerate from men.

From makeover shows, I learned that I was ugly. From romantic comedies, I learned that stalking means he loves you and persistence means he earned you — and also that I was ugly. From Disney movies, I learned that if I made my waist small enough (maybe with the help of a witch), a man or large hog-bear might marry me, and that's where my story would end. "The Smurfs" taught me that boys can have distinct personalities, like being smart or grumpy, and girls can have only one (that personality is "high heels"). From "The Breakfast Club," I learned that rage and degradation are the selling points of an alluring bad boy, not the red flags of an abuser. From pretty much all media, I learned that complicated women are "crazy" and complicated men are geniuses.

That's essentially a random sample, and pulled from media I actually like. You could make a parallel list about race, sexuality, ability, poverty — every vector of identity that has historically been funneled through, for instance, the 82.4 percent of film directors who are white men (according to a 2015 report by the Directors Guild of America).

Do you know how noise-canceling headphones work? (I don't really, but I'm going to embarrass myself for the sake of the metaphor.) They have a built-in microphone that measures the ambient noise around you, then generates an exact inversion of that sound wave and adds it to the mix in your headphones. When a frequency meets its opposite — when the peaks of one match up with the valleys of another — the result is called phase cancellation. The two waves cancel each other out. Silence.

What we could really use from Hollywood is about 100 years of phase cancellation.

We need new work that actively challenges and counterbalances old assumptions, that offers radical models for how to conceive of ourselves and how to treat each other. We need artists and studios fighting for diverse work made by diverse creators for diverse audiences because it's the right thing to do, not just because "Black Panther" is hurtling toward a possible billion-dollar worldwide box-office take. Capitalism won't germinate that kind of pure morality on its own, but we can choose it. If we really want to have this #MeToo reckoning — if we want to fix what's broken — those choices are part of it. The movement can't just disrupt the culture; it has to become the culture.

One of the most breathtaking things about #MeToo — just behind the iron-jawed fury of its deponents — is how swiftly and decisively it pulled conversations about sexual predation from the conceptual to the concrete. After decades of debates and doubts and dissertations and settlements and nondisclosure agreements and whisper networks and stasis and silence, all of a sudden, in one great gust, powerful men are toppling. Talk has become action. The seemingly untouchable have lost jobs, reputations and legacies overnight. Choices have consequences, even if you are Harvey Weinstein. This is new.

But in the rush of catharsis, it's important not to lose track of some of those old conceptual conversations, because we never came close to finishing them. We are not done talking about why so many men feel entitled to space, power and other people's bodies. We are not done talking about our culture's hostility toward women's sexual pleasure. We are not done talking about how to get justice for "imperfect" victims, and how to let go of perpetrators we love. We are not done talking about how to decide which abusers deserve a path to redemption, and what that path might look like. We are not done talking about the legal system. We are not done talking about sex. We are not done talking about race.

Unseating a couple (or a score, or even a generation) of powerful abusers is a start, but it's not an end, unless we also radically change the power structure that selects their replacements and the shared values that remain even when the movement wanes. Art didn't invent oppressive gender roles, racial stereotyping or rape culture, but it reflects, polishes and sells them back to us every moment of our waking lives. We make art, and it simultaneously makes us. Shouldn't it follow, then, that we can change ourselves by changing the art we make?

**LINDY WEST** is the author of "Shrill: Notes From a Loud Woman" and a contributing opinion writer.

# The Stars of 'Black Panther' Waited a Lifetime for This Moment

BY REGGIE UGWU | FEB. 12, 2018

FOR ALL ITS SCI-FI SPARKLE and requisite fate-of-the-world stakes, the most salient aspects of Marvel Studios' "Black Panther" may be the most basic: It is the first major superhero movie with an African protagonist; the first to star a majority black cast; and in Ryan Coogler ("Creed," "Fruitvale Station"), the first to employ a black writer and director.

Those distinctions may add up to a public relations victory for the blockbuster factory responsible for "The Avengers" and the rest of the $13 billion Marvel Cinematic Universe, but it's a mixed one — to count the film's racial milestones is to acknowledge the homogeneity of its predecessors. (There have been 17, since we're counting.)

As often happened in the comic books, however, the house that "Iron Man" built can ably dismantle the very norms it once codified. And in that sense, "Black Panther" may punctuate an emerging trend. It follows the mold-breaking work of James Gunn's stylish "Guardians of the Galaxy" movies and Taika Waititi's self-aware "Thor: Ragnarok," suggesting — after 10 years of Tony Stark — that Marvel's tolerance for risk might be growing along with its financial clout.

"Black Panther" is also, of course, a shrewd bet on the social and economic muscle of black filmgoers. Mr. Coogler's film, based on an unsung 1960s creation of Stan Lee and Jack Kirby, has inspired a level of anticipation that wildly exceeds the name recognition of its title character — owing, in part, to pent-up demand for a megabudget movie devoted to black life.

As with "Wonder Woman" last year, another movie that spoke to an underserved population at a moment of acute political anxiety, audiences have reacted with partisan fervor.

"Black Panther" is already a phenomenon on social media, where eager fans are teasing their opening-night outfits, ruminating on race and representation with the hashtag #WhatBlackPantherMeansToMe and showing their support for the #BlackPantherChallenge (a spontaneous campaign to buy tickets and popcorn for children). The film recently broke the advance ticket sales record for any movie released in the first quarter, according to the online vendor Fandango, surpassing "The Hunger Games" and the 2017 live-action remake of "Beauty and the Beast."

The morning after a red-carpet premiere in Hollywood last month that left Twitter swooning, the stars, director and producer of the film gathered for a spirited conversation about their role in challenging standard depictions of the African diaspora on screen.

Taking part in the discussion were Mr. Coogler; Chadwick Boseman, who plays T'Challa, a.k.a. Black Panther, king of the fictional African nation of Wakanda; Lupita Nyong'o (Nakia, a Wakandan spy and T'Challa's love interest); Michael B. Jordan (Erik Killmonger, an African-American adversary of Black Panther's); Danai Gurira (Okoye, Wakanda's greatest warrior); and Kevin Feige, a producer of "Black Panther" and president of Marvel Studios. These are edited excerpts from the conversation.

*I read a funny tweet the other day that said this movie is basically reparations.*

[Rolling laughter]

**Chadwick Boseman** I still want my reparations! I still want my reparations!

**Ryan Coogler** [laughing] I think only reparations can be reparations.

*It's silly, but is there a kernel of truth there for any of you? The idea that Disney and Marvel investing so much in a movie with a black cast and crew can count as something like restitution?*

**Danai Gurira** What it does in such a beautiful way, to me, is it sets a precedent. We've read a lot of subtitles for German and Russian — we can read subtitles for African languages now. People can't go back and say, "No, that's going to be too hard, it's Africa." They can't do that. And that is so thrilling to me.

**Michael B. Jordan** It couldn't have been done on a bigger level. If Marvel is behind it, then it's gotta be O.K. Moving forward, everybody's going to start to have the courage to tell bold stories that people didn't think were lucrative, didn't think that anybody wanted to see. All of that, I feel, is getting ready to dissolve.

**Boseman** It has to.

**Gurira** No, it will.

**Coogler** What I'll say is, this is my second time working in the studio system, and they say it's the studio system, but it's really the people system. It's who's running the studio? How are they running it? When you look at Disney with [Tendo Nagenda, executive vice president for production at Walt Disney Studios, and Nate Moore, a producer at Marvel Studios and an executive producer of "Black Panther"], it's a place that's interested in representation, not just for the sake of representation, but representation because that's what works, that's what's going to make quality stuff that the world is going to embrace, that's what leads to success.

*Kevin, there's long been this idea in Hollywood that movies with black casts don't perform well internationally. Does that end with "Black Panther"?*

**Kevin Feige** I certainly hope so. One thing I would always remind Ryan of when we would talk about humor and entertainment value in the film was that the biggest statement this movie can make is to be a success around the globe. And I think he's delivered a movie that's going to do that, and that disproves [beliefs] that had maybe never been true but had never been tested.

*For the actors, what did joining this film mean to you and how did it feel different from other movies you've done?*

**Boseman** I've done other films that have had historic significance because of what has happened in the past, but this not only refers to the past, it sets the stage for where we're going.

**Gurira** I've had a passion for telling African stories for a really long time, being American-born and Zimbabwe-raised. That biculturalism is something that I try to address in my work as a playwright [her 2016 drama "Eclipsed" was nominated for a Tony for best play], but nothing can address it like a Marvel movie. I had a childlike glee after my meeting with Ryan — I kind of floated around, found my car somehow. You think you're alone in the struggle until you meet someone and then you think, "Oh wow, we're all in it together? And y'all are doing this already? And I just have to be in it?" It was just so beautiful.

**Lupita Nyong'o** Seeing it yesterday, I'm even more excited about the celebration of pan-Africanism, because this movie is really about a contemporary Africa relating very intimately with a contemporary America via the characters of Black Panther and Killmonger. We're talking about some really deep issues that we don't often voice but we all feel. [Ms. Nyong'o was born in Mexico to Kenyan parents and raised in Kenya.]

**Boseman** A lot of times, being [a black man] in Hollywood, when you get material you'll read it and you'll be like, "That's not us." When I got the initial call from Kevin Feige, my hope was that they would have the courage to give Black Panther its true essence and put somebody behind it that would have my same passion for what it could be. And they did that.

*On set, did you have that feeling of "This is important" or did you just try to do good work like normal?*

**Coogler** I learned a skill from playing football. I was a wide receiver — they throw you the ball, you can't drop it. So I learned that you gotta tune everything else out.

If I get to set and there's a hundred black people on the side of a waterfall and Lupita is dressed in this adornment and Danai is dressed in this adornment and they're like, "Hey Ryan, do I stand here or here?" I can't think, "Ah, this is amazing, I'm making 'Black Panther' and there's all these black folks on screen!" I really gotta tell Danai that she needs to move over here, and I gotta tell her five reasons why she's gotta move over here, because she's gonna wanna know 'em! [Laughter]

But seriously, I grew up reading these comic books and watching all these movies. If I really thought about the fact that I'm making one of these things right now, with people I know and love, I would break down emotionally. I wouldn't be no good to anybody.

**Nyong'o** A moment when I really felt a vibration was when we were shooting [the waterfall scene]. There were hundreds of extras and we were all in these traditional clothes and there were all the tribal colors and drumming, and between takes, the drummers started riffing to [Snoop Dogg's] "Drop It Like It's Hot." The whole crowd started to go [sings the melody] and we were all dancing as Ryan figured things out below.

In that moment, I was like, "This is big." I had never been on a set with so many black people before and we were all so focused and I could feel a vibration in the air. We all felt so privileged to have an opportunity to be a part of this moment in history.

*Michael, one of the interesting complexities of the film comes from Killmonger's identity as an African-American, which contrasts against T'Challa's African-ness. What did you want to bring to the character?*

**Jordan** Ryan [and I] started getting into the back story of where he came from and how his upbringing really affected his personality, his outlook, his rage, his agenda. We felt like we could show where Erik is coming from and make people feel why he is so angry, why he is so lost. He doesn't know who he is, but he knows the answers are out there.

**Boseman** For me, [Killmonger and T'Challa] are two sides of the same coin — African and African-American. As an African-American, if you're disconnected from your ancestry and your past, you have this conflict that comes from that and so there is a healing experience that is possible because of that.

**Coogler** The fracture that Killmonger has, that's the fracture I lived with my whole life. I'm from a place that I'd never been to and that nobody who I loved had been to because they couldn't afford to go [to Africa. Mr. Coogler grew up in Richmond in Northern California]. So I would hear stories from them about this place that they didn't even know anything about, and those stories were a counterbalance to the awful things that we did hear about them.

*In the movie, Wakanda disguises vast technological resources from the world, and white people who aren't in the know refer to it dismissively as a primitive backwater. That's a very real view that a lot of people hold about Africa, as recent comments attributed to the president made clear. What do you hope will be the effect of introducing audiences to this counternarrative about the continent?*

**Coogler** The narrative about the continent that we know is actually a fairly recent narrative, if you think about human history. It's a narrative that was born out of what happened when the countries of Africa were conquered.

But the truth is that some of those places that people might refer to as backwaters — and these recent comments definitely aren't the first time somebody has said something like that — were the cradle of civilization. They were the first places to do anything that we would consider to be civilized.

All the structures that we built in Wakanda, they're taller structures of what you'll find in Africa. Some of them we switched up — instead of mud we used [the fictional supermetal] vibranium — but those are buildings that you'll really find in Mali, in Ethiopia, in Nigeria.

I spent about three weeks in Africa [doing research for "Black Panther"] and I truly felt that seeing it for myself was necessary for my growth as a human being. That experience made me not only capable [of writing] this film, but it made me whole as a person.

# With 'There There,' Tommy Orange Has Written a New Kind of American Epic

BY ALEXANDRA ALTER | MAY 31, 2018

"THERE THERE," Tommy Orange's polyphonic debut novel, takes its title from Gertrude Stein's cutting line about Oakland, Calif: "There is no there there."

Mr. Orange, who grew up in Oakland and is a member of the Cheyenne and Arapaho tribes, uses that concave, twisty riddle as his novel's recurring anthem, a shorthand to describe the disorienting experience of living in America as a self-described "urban Indian."

For native people, Mr. Orange writes, cities and towns themselves represent the absence of a homeland — a lost world of "buried ancestral land, glass and concrete and wire and steel, unreturnable covered memory. There is no there there."

Mr. Orange, 36, seems at home with those sorts of paradoxes and contradictions. He grew up straddling two worlds, never quite feeling like he belonged. His father, who spoke Cheyenne as his first language, was a Native American Church ceremony leader. His white mother, a wandering hippie and spiritual seeker, later converted to evangelical Christianity and denounced his father's religious practices as demonic. Mr. Orange wasn't sure what to believe — as a boy, he used to worry about the coming apocalypse and spending eternity in hellfire.

With the highly anticipated "There There," which Knopf will publish next week, Mr. Orange has written a new kind of Native American epic, one that reflects his ambivalence and the complexity of his upbringing. "There's been a lot of reservation literature written," he said. "I wanted to have my characters struggle in the way that I struggled, and the way that I see other native people struggle, with identity and with authenticity."

Tommy Orange, seen here at the Indian American Institute of Art in Santa Fe, N.M.

"There There," which follows a dozen Native American characters whose lives converge at a big powwow at the Oakland Coliseum, has drawn accolades from writers like Louise Erdrich, Margaret Atwood, Marlon James and Pam Houston. "This book is going to remake the literary canon, and not just the native canon," said Ms. Houston, one of Mr. Orange's teachers at the Institute of American Indian Arts in Santa Fe, N.M.

Mr. Orange is part of a new generation of acclaimed indigenous writers from the United States and Canada who are publishing groundbreaking, formally innovative poetry, fiction and prose, shattering old tropes and stereotypes about Native American literature, experience and identity. Their ranks include poets like Layli Long Soldier, Natalie Diaz, Joshua Whitehead and Tommy Pico, and the essayists and memoirists Elissa Washuta and Terese Marie Mailhot.

These writers are radically reshaping the native canon, with stylistically and thematically diverse works that reflect a broad range of influences, from pop culture and hip-hop in Mr. Pico's poetry, to cyberpunk dystopian science fiction in Mr. Whitehead's collection, "Full-Metal Indigiqueer."

"All these writers are doing something very contemporary, which feels important because of how historical it's always felt," Mr. Orange said. "A lot of this writing is modern, it's trying to break and bend boundaries."

Some are consciously deploying painful stereotypes, and subverting them. Mr. Orange opens his novel with a meditation on the symbolism of the Indian head — an image that appears on coins, flags and team uniforms as seemingly benign décor, but also recalls centuries of violence against indigenous people, tracing back to 17th century massacres when the heads of slaughtered native people were displayed on spikes.

Mr. Pico, 34, who grew up on the Viejas Indian reservation of the Kumeyaay Nation in Southern California, refers to indigenous people in his poems with the letters "NDN" — an insider shorthand for "Indian." Nonnative people who pick up his poems are often confused by the term at first, but indigenous people get it right away, he said.

"The term 'Indian' was an imposed identity on a group of myriad indigenous people that amassed us into one, as a way to rob us of our distinctions," said Mr. Pico, who lives in Brooklyn and recently published "Junk," his third volume of poetry. "I saw an opportunity to take something that had been imposed on us and to create a new identity out of it, one that only we were familiar with."

In her memoir, "Heart Berries," Ms. Mailhot, 34, who grew up on the Seabird Island Reservation in British Columbia, uses the word "squaw," co-opting the stereotype to highlight how Indian women are often objectified, sexualized and dismissed. "I feel like a squaw," she writes. "The type white people imagine: a feral thing with greasy hair."

Ms. Mailhot and Mr. Orange are both recent graduates of the Institute of American Indian Arts. The school's graduate writing program, which was founded in 2013, is largely staffed by and designed for native writers, and has become an incubator of sorts for new native voices, among them the poets b. william bearhart and Chee Brossy and the poet and nonfiction writer Sasha LaPointe. The program has been a catalyst behind what some are calling another Native Renaissance — a proliferation of new literature that mirrors the arrival of acclaimed indigenous writers like Ms. Erdrich, Joy Harjo and Leslie Marmon Silko in the 1970s and 1980s.

"At I.A.I.A., I felt we were building an aesthetic," Ms. Mailhot said. 'We're not interested in rewriting what's already out there."

After graduating and selling their books, Ms. Mailhot and Mr. Orange both decided to teach at I.A.I.A. The task feels even more vital following the allegations of sexual harassment and misconduct against the novelist Sherman Alexie, who was deeply involved with the program and often championed the work of younger writers. (After Mr. Alexie was accused of harassment by multiple women, both Mr. Orange and Ms. Mailhot asked their publishers to remove his endorsements from their books.)

The accusations against Mr. Alexie, who is perhaps the most prominent contemporary Native American writer, were painful for his former students and other young indigenous writers who looked up to him. But the scandal and its aftermath also had an unexpected positive side effect: Other native writers were ready to step in and become mentors and teachers.

"I want to help build momentum and get more native voices out there," Mr. Orange said. "It's a really powerful thing to be part of a native writing community."

Growing up in Oakland, Mr. Orange, who is boyish looking with close cropped hair and a round, freckled face, often felt out of place. At his mostly white high school, he was called racial slurs — not for being native, but because kids mistook him for Chinese. Other times, people assumed he was Mexican.

His parents, who met at a commune in New Mexico, fought a lot after his mother converted to evangelical Christianity, and eventually divorced. (Years later, his mother returned to the Native American Church).

Mr. Orange often didn't feel Native American enough, or white enough, he said. He threw himself into roller hockey, and fell in love with music after getting a guitar for his 18th birthday. He studied sound art in college, and hoped to one day compose piano scores for movies, but job prospects in the field were slim. After graduating in 2004, he found work at a used bookstore, and became a voracious reader, devouring books by Borges and Kafka and John Kennedy Toole.

He bounced around between jobs for a while, waiting tables in New Mexico and working at a Native American health center in California, reading and writing as much as he could. In 2010, he had the idea for "There There" while driving to Los Angeles to go to a piano concert.

He envisioned a narrative with a large cast of characters, partly as a way to address how little has been written about the lives of urban Native Americans, who account for the majority of indigenous people living in the United States.

Mr. Orange struggled for several years with the structure, puzzling over how the characters' lives fit together, and discarded hundreds of pages and entire chapters delving into different characters' family histories. Eventually, he settled on an unconventional form: The novel opens with a series of brief and jarring vignettes revealing the violence and genocide that indigenous people have endured, and how it has been sanitized over the centuries.

Mr. Orange said he felt like he couldn't move the story forward without first going back.

"As native writers, there's a certain feeling that you have to set the record straight before you even begin," he said. "It's been told wrong, and not told, so often."

# For Some Viewers, 'Crazy Rich Asians' Is Not Asian Enough

BY MIKE IVES | AUG. 16, 2018

HONG KONG — "Crazy Rich Asians," a romantic comedy that opened in the United States on Wednesday, is a rare commodity: a Hollywood film with a majority Asian cast. For many Asian-American viewers, that is a positive, if sorely belated, development.

But ahead of the film's release next week in Singapore, where much of the action is set, some residents there have questioned whether "Crazy Rich Asians" is the panacea of diversity that its proponents suggest.

A primary worry is that the Warner Bros. film focuses on Singapore's Chinese, the dominant ethnic majority, at the expense of Malays, Indians and other ethnic minorities who collectively account for about a quarter of Singapore's 5.6 million people.

"Part of the way that this movie is being sold to everyone is as this big win for diversity, as this representative juggernaut, as this great Asian hope," said Sangeetha Thanapal, a Singaporean Indian writer and activist who is researching a doctoral dissertation on the concept of Chinese privilege in Singapore.

"I think that's really problematic because if you're going to sell yourself as that, then you bloody better actually have actual representation" of Singaporean minorities, she said.

The film's detractors said that because "Crazy Rich Asians" had not yet been released in their hometown, their criticisms were based on the film's trailer and marketing campaign.

In a statement posted on Twitter last month, Constance Wu, the film's female lead, indirectly addressed the criticism by acknowledging that the film "won't represent every Asian American."

"So for those who don't feel seen, I hope there is a story you find soon that does represent you," Ms. Wu added. "I am rooting for you."

Janice Chua, a producer on the film, initially agreed to comment, but later said she was unavailable. A spokeswoman for Warner Bros. did not respond on the record to questions about the film.

"Crazy Rich Asians" is based on a novel by Kevin Kwan that satirizes Singapore's megarich, and the film's trailer oozes with luxury cars, opulent parties and other trappings of the One Percent.

The film is "an unabashed celebration of luxury and money, with hints of class conflict that have more to do with aspiration than envy or anger, set in an Asia miraculously free of history or politics," the film critic A. O. Scott wrote in The New York Times.

Kevin Ma, the founder of Asia in Cinema, a Hong Kong-based news site, said that the film's emphasis on over-the-top wealth was not surprising. "It's not a new thing for Asians to see rich Asians on screen," he said.

Other critics have applauded the inclusion of cast members who are not of East Asian descent. The cast includes the Filipino-American actor Nico Santos, and Henry Golding, the male lead, who has an English father and a mother from Malaysia's Iban indigenous group.

Some Singaporean writers said they feared the film would mirror the underrepresentation of minorities that already pervades local films and television shows.

"Mind you, I'm happy that there are non-East Asian actors involved in major roles," said Ng Yi-Sheng, an author and gay rights activist whose debut poetry collection won the 2008 Singapore Literature Prize.

"But judging from the trailers, the browner Asian characters are predominantly guards and domestic workers and drivers," Mr. Ng said in an email. "That's kind of oppressive, don't you think?"

Singapore, a financial hub at the southern tip of the Malay Peninsula, is a former British colony that gained independence as part of Malaysia in 1963 and then split from Malaysia two years later. The city-state's governing party has never lost its hold on power, and the government controls the domestic news media.

Even though Singapore's Chinese ethnic majority accounts for about three-quarters of the city-state's population, the government often goes to great lengths to promote interethnic harmony as a symbol of national identity.

"We don't really have enough of a precolonial culture to celebrate — we're on Malay land, but most of us aren't Malay, and Chinese culture was a little too Communist-affiliated in the old days," Mr. Ng said. "So a multiracial concept of nationhood was kind of the obvious choice for us."

But it has always been a delicate balancing act. Today, there are growing concerns in Singapore that a newly powerful China could upset that equilibrium by seeking to promote loyalty to the Chinese "motherland" among Singaporean Chinese.

In the local film industry, the concern centers on why minority actors are "seldom featured as leads in movies and sometimes assigned stereotypical roles," said Mathew Mathews, a senior research fellow at the Institute of Policy Studies, a Singaporean research institute.

Last year, for example, the Singaporean Indian actor Shrey Bhargava wrote on Facebook that he had been asked in an audition to use a stereotypical Indian accent.

Mr. Bhargava said he had left feeling disgusted and had concluded that diversity in Singaporean films "comes down to playing stereotypes so the majority race can find it amusing." His post went viral and sparked a debate about ethnicity and diversity.

But Mr. Mathews, who has studied race, religion and immigration in Singapore, played down the debate over ethnic representation in "Crazy Rich Asians."

"I think most fair-minded Singaporeans would see this film as a work of fiction and not expect a high level of realism and accuracy in cultural portrayals," he said in an email.

The film's detractors disagree.

Alfian Sa'at, a prominent Singaporean author, who writes in English and Malay, said in a scathing Facebook post that the film featured "East Asian people purporting to speak for all Asians," adding that he hoped it would "go away quietly."

And in a Twitter thread and a Medium essay, Kirsten Han, a Singaporean journalist and activist, offered an equally blistering critique.

"When it comes to representation, what I would like to see as a Singaporean is something that reflects my country and society in all our diversity and complexity, and helps audiences make connections between our experiences and theirs," Ms. Han wrote in the essay.

" 'Crazy Rich Asians' does nothing to improve the situation," she added.

## CHAPTER 4

# The Alt-Right and White Identity

One of the ways in which identity politics has resurged on the political right is through the rise of the so-called alt-right. Even the term "alt-right" is controversial, with some people arguing that this name glosses over the extremist motivations of the group. According to the Anti-Defamation League, "alt-right" is a "vague term actually encompass[ing] a range of people on the extreme right who reject mainstream conservatism in favor of forms of conservatism that embrace implicit or explicit racism or white supremacy." Critics of this term prefer more descriptive names like white supremacism, antifeminism and neo-Nazism.

## Alt-Right, Alt-Left, Antifa: A Glossary of Extremist Language

**BY LIAM STACK | AUG. 15, 2017**

PRESIDENT TRUMP ANGRILY denounced the so-called alt-left at a news conference on Tuesday, claiming that the group attacked followers of the so-called alt-right at a white supremacist rally that exploded into deadly violence in Charlottesville, Va., on Saturday.

"What about the 'alt-left' that came charging at the, as you say, the 'alt-right'? Do they have any semblance of guilt?" he asked. There was "blame on both sides," he said. "I have no doubt about it."

Both phrases are part of a broad lexicon of far-right terminology that has become important to understanding American politics during the Trump administration. Many of these terms have their roots in movements that are racist, anti-Semitic and sexist.

Here is a brief guide to the meaning of those expressions and others used by white supremacists and far-right extremists.

## ALT-RIGHT

The "alt-right" is a racist, far-right movement based on an ideology of white nationalism and anti-Semitism. Many news organizations do not use the term, preferring terms like "white nationalism" and "far right."

The movement's self-professed goal is the creation of a white state and the destruction of "leftism," which it calls "an ideology of death." Richard B. Spencer, a leader in the movement, has described the movement as "identity politics for white people."

It is also anti-immigrant, anti-feminist and opposed to homosexuality and gay and transgender rights. It is highly decentralized but has a wide online presence, where its ideology is spread via racist or sexist memes with a satirical edge.

It believes that higher education is "only appropriate for a cognitive elite" and that most citizens should be educated in trade schools or apprenticeships.

## ALT-LEFT

Researchers who study extremist groups in the United States say there is no such thing as the "alt-left." Mark Pitcavage, an analyst at the Anti-Defamation League, said the word had been made up to create a false equivalence between the far right and "anything vaguely left-seeming that they didn't like."

Some centrist liberals have taken to using this term.

"It did not arise organically, and it refers to no actual group or movement or network," Mr. Pitcavage said in an email. "It's just a made-up epithet, similar to certain people calling any news they don't like 'fake news.' "

On Tuesday, Mr. Trump said the "alt-left" was partly to blame for the Charlottesville violence, during which a counterprotester, Heather D. Heyer, was killed.

### ALT-LIGHT

The "alt-light" comprises members of the far right who once fell under the "alt-right" umbrella but have since split from the group because, by and large, racism and anti-Semitism are not central to its far-right nationalist views, according to Ryan Lenz, the editor of Hatewatch, a publication of the Southern Poverty Law Center. Members of the alt-right mocked these dissidents as "the alt-light."

"The alt-light is the alt-right without the racist overtones, but it is hard to differentiate it sometimes because you're looking at people who sometimes dance between both camps," he said.

A white supremacist militia at the rally in Charlottesville on Saturday.

The two groups often feud online over "the Jewish Question," or whether Jews profit by secretly manipulating the government and news media.

## ANTIFA

"Antifa" is a contraction of the word "anti-fascist." It was coined in Germany in the 1960s and 1970s by a network of groups that spread across Europe to confront right-wing extremists, according to Mr. Pitcavage. A similar movement was seen in the 1980s in the United States and has re-emerged recently as the "alt-right" has risen to prominence.

For some so-called antifa members, the goal is to physically confront white supremacists. "If they can get at them, to assault them and engage in street fighting," Mr. Pitcavage said. Mr. Lenz, at the Southern Poverty Law Center, called the group "an old left-wing extremist movement."

Members of the "alt-right" broadly portray protesters who oppose them as "antifa," or the "alt-left," and say they bear some responsibility for any violence that ensues — a claim made by Mr. Trump on Tuesday.

But analysts said comparing antifa with neo-Nazi or white supremacist protesters was a false equivalence.

## CUCK

"Cuck" is an insult used by the "alt-right" to attack the masculinity of an opponent, originally other conservatives, whom the movement deemed insufficiently committed to racism and anti-Semitism.

It is short for "cuckold," a word dating back to the Middle Ages that describes a man who knows his wife is sleeping with other men and does not object. Mr. Lenz said the use of the word by the "alt-right" often had racial overtones.

## S.J.W.

S.J.W. is short for "social justice warrior" and is used by the right as an epithet for someone who advocates liberal causes like feminism, racial justice or gay and transgender rights. It is also sometimes used to imply that a person's online advocacy of a cause is insincere or done for appearances. It became widely used during "GamerGate," a controversy that began in 2014 over sexism in video game subcultures.

Mr. Lenz, whose organization has specific criteria for which groups it classifies as Nazi organizations, said the right used the phrase "to rhetorically address the fact that the left sometimes calls anyone who disagrees with it Nazis." He said the alt-right had created the term so its followers had a similar blanket term to deride the left.

## BLOOD AND SOIL

Video taken at the white supremacist rally in Charlottesville on Saturday showed marchers chanting "blood and soil." The phrase is a 19th-century German nationalist term that connotes a mystical bond between the blood of an ethnic group and the soil of their country.

It was used as a Nazi slogan in Germany during the 1930s and 1940s and since then "has been transported to neo-Nazi groups and other white supremacists around the world," Mr. Pitcavage said. It is one of several Nazi symbols that have been adopted as a slogan by some members of the "alt-right."

## GLOBALISM

Globalism is sometimes used as a synonym for globalization, the network of economic interconnection that became the dominant international system after the Cold War. The word has become more commonly used since Mr. Trump railed against globalism frequently on the campaign trail.

For the far right, globalism has long had distinct xenophobic, anti-immigrant and anti-Semitic overtones. It refers to a conspiratorial worldview: a cabal that likes open borders, diversity and weak nation states, and that dislikes white people, Christianity and the traditional culture of their own country.

## WHITE GENOCIDE

White genocide is a white nationalist belief that white people, as a race, are endangered and face extinction as a result of nonwhite immigration and marriage between the races, a process being manipulated by Jews, according to Mr. Lenz. It is the underlying concept behind far-right, anti-immigration arguments, especially those aimed at immigrants who are not white Christians.

The concept was popularized by Bob Whitaker, a former economics professor and Reagan appointee to the Office of Personnel Management, who wrote a 221-word "mantra" on the subject that ended with the rallying cry: "Anti-racist is code word for anti-white."

Mr. Pitcavage said the concept of white genocide was often communicated online through a white supremacist saying called the Fourteen Words: "We must secure the existence of our people and a future for white children."

The saying was created by David Lane, a white supremacist sentenced to 190 years in prison in connection with the 1984 murder of the Jewish radio host Alan Berg.

# A Voice of Hate in America's Heartland

BY RICHARD FAUSSET | NOV. 25, 2017

HUBER HEIGHTS, OHIO — Tony and Maria Hovater were married this fall. They registered at Target. On their list was a muffin pan, a four-drawer dresser and a pineapple slicer.

Ms. Hovater, 25, was worried about Antifa bashing up the ceremony. Weddings are hard enough to plan for when your fiancé is not an avowed white nationalist.

But Mr. Hovater, in the days leading up to the wedding, was somewhat less anxious. There are times when it can feel toxic to openly identify as a far-right extremist in the Ohio of 2017. But not always. He said the election of President Trump helped open a space for people like him, demonstrating that it is not the end of the world to be attacked as the

GEORGE ETHEREDGE FOR THE NEW YORK TIMES

Tony Hovater at his home in New Carlisle, Ohio.

bigot he surely is: "You can just say, 'Yeah, so?' And move on."

It was a weeknight at Applebee's in Huber Heights, a suburb of Dayton, a few weeks before the wedding. The couple, who live in nearby New Carlisle, were shoulder to shoulder at a table, young and in love. He was in a plain T-shirt, she in a sleeveless jean jacket. She ordered the boneless wings. Her parents had met him, she said, and approved of the match. The wedding would be small. Some of her best friends were going to be there. "A lot of girls are not really into politics," she said.

In Ohio, amid the row crops and rolling hills, the Olive Gardens and Steak 'n Shakes, Mr. Hovater's presence can make hardly a ripple. He is the Nazi sympathizer next door, polite and low-key at a time the old boundaries of accepted political activity can seem alarmingly in flux. Most Americans would be disgusted and baffled by his casually approving remarks about Hitler, disdain for democracy and belief that the races are better off separate. But his tattoos are innocuous pop-culture references: a slice of cherry pie adorns one arm, a homage to the TV show "Twin Peaks." He says he prefers to spread the gospel of white nationalism with satire. He is a big "Seinfeld" fan.

"I guess it seems weird when talking about these type of things," he says. "You know, I'm coming at it in a mid-90s, Jewish, New York, observational-humor way."

Mr. Hovater, 29, is a welder by trade. He is not a star among the resurgent radical American right so much as a committed foot soldier — an organizer, an occasional podcast guest on a website called Radio Aryan, and a self-described "social media villain," although, in person, his Midwestern manners would please anyone's mother. In 2015, he helped start the Traditionalist Worker Party, one of the extreme right-wing groups that marched in Charlottesville, Va., in August, and again at a "White Lives Matter" rally last month in Tennessee. The group's stated mission is to "fight for the interests of White Americans."

A bookshelf at Mr. Hovater's house.

Its leaders claim to oppose racism, though the Anti-Defamation League says the group "has participated in white supremacist events all over the country." On its website, a swastika armband goes for $20.

If the Charlottesville rally came as a shock, with hundreds of white Americans marching in support of ideologies many have long considered too vile, dangerous or stupid to enter the political mainstream, it obscured the fact that some in the small, loosely defined alt-right movement are hoping to make those ideas seem less than shocking for the "normies," or normal people, that its sympathizers have tended to mock online.

And to go from mocking to wooing, the movement will be looking to make use of people like the Hovaters and their trappings of normie life — their fondness for National Public Radio, their four cats, their bridal registry.

"We need to have more families. We need to be able to just be normal," said Matthew Heimbach, the leader of the Traditionalist Worker

Party, in a podcast conversation with Mr. Hovater. Why, he asked self-mockingly, were so many followers "abnormal"?

Mr. Hovater replied: "I mean honestly, it takes people with, like, sort of an odd view of life, at first, to come this way. Because most people are pacified really easy, you know. Like, here's some money, here's a nice TV, go watch your sports, you know?"

He added: "The fact that we're seeing more and more normal people come is because things have gotten so bad. And if they keep getting worse, we'll keep getting more, just, normal people."

## FLATTENING THE EDGES

Mr. Hovater's face is narrow and punctuated with sharply peaked eyebrows, like a pair of air quotes, and he tends to deliver his favorite adjective, "edgy," with a flat affect and maximum sarcastic intent. It is a sort of implicit running assertion that the edges of acceptable American political discourse — edges set by previous generations, like the one that fought the Nazis — are laughable.

"I don't want you to think I'm some 'edgy' Republican," he says, while flatly denouncing the concept of democracy.

"I don't even think those things should be 'edgy,' " he says, while defending his assertion that Jews run the worlds of finance and the media, and "appear to be working more in line with their own interests than everybody else's."

His political evolution — from vaguely leftist rock musician to ardent libertarian to fascist activist — was largely fueled by the kinds of frustrations that would not seem exotic to most American conservatives. He believes the federal government is too big, the news media is biased, and that affirmative action programs for minorities are fundamentally unfair.

Ask him how he moved so far right, and he declares that public discourse has become "so toxic that there's no way to effectively lobby for interests that involve white people." He name-drops Murray Rothbard and Hans-Hermann Hoppe, architects of "anarcho-capitalism," with its idea that free markets serve as better societal regulators than the state. And he refers to the 2013 science-fiction movie "Pacific Rim," in which society is attacked by massive monsters that emerge from beneath the Pacific Ocean.

"So the people, they don't ask the monsters to stop," he says. "They build a giant robot to try to stop them. And that's essentially what fascism is. It's like our version of centrally coming together to try to stop another already centralized force."

Mr. Hovater grew up on integrated Army bases and attended a mostly white Ohio high school. He did not want for anything. He experienced no scarring racial episodes. His parents, he says, were the kinds of people who "always assume things aren't going well. But they don't necessarily know why."

He is adamant that the races are probably better off separated, but he insists he is not racist. He is a white nationalist, he says, not a white supremacist. There were mixed-race couples at the wedding.

Mr. Hovater and others in the loosely-defined alt-right movement are hoping to make their ideas less than shocking.

Mr. Hovater said he was fine with it. "That's their thing, man," he said.

Online it is uglier. On Facebook, Mr. Hovater posted a picture purporting to show what life would have looked like if Germany had won World War II: a streetscape full of happy white people, a bustling American-style diner and swastikas everywhere.

"What part is supposed to look unappealing?" he wrote.

In an essay lamenting libertarianism's leftward drift, he wrote: "At this rate I'm sure the presidential candidate they'll put up in a few cycles will be an overweight, black, crippled dyke with dyslexia."

After he attended the Charlottesville rally, in which a white nationalist plowed his car into a group of left-wing protesters, killing one of them, Mr. Hovater wrote that he was proud of the comrades who joined him there: "We made history. Hail victory."

In German, "Hail victory" is "Sieg heil."

## A GROWING MOVEMENT

Before white nationalism, his world was heavy metal. He played drums in two bands, and his embrace of fascism, on the surface, shares some traits with the hipster's cooler-than-thou quest for the most extreme of musical subgenres. Online, he and his allies can also give the impression that their movement is one big laugh — an enormous trolling event put on by self-mocking, politically incorrect kids playing around on the ash heap of history.

On the party's website, the swastika armband is formally listed as a "NSDAP LARP Armband." NSDAP was the abbreviation for Hitler's Nazi Party. LARP stands for "Live-Action Role Playing," a term originally meant to describe fantasy fans who dress up as wizards and warlocks.

But the movement is no joke. The party, Mr. Hovater said, is now approaching 1,000 people. He said that it has held food and school-supply drives in Appalachia. "These are people that the establishment doesn't care about," he said.

Marilyn Mayo, a senior research fellow at the Anti-Defamation League's Center on Extremism, estimated that the Traditionalist Worker Party had a few hundred members at most, while Americans who identify as "alt-right" could number in the tens of thousands.

"It is small in the grand scheme of things, but it's one of the segments of the white supremacist movement that's grown over the last two years," she said.

It was midday at a Panera Bread, and Mr. Hovater was describing his political awakening over a turkey sandwich. He mentioned books by Charles Murray and Pat Buchanan. He talked about his presence on 4chan, the online message board and alt-right breeding ground ("That's where the scary memes come from," he deadpanned). He spoke dispassionately about the injustice of affirmative action, about the "malice directed toward white people" in popular media, about how the cartoon comedy "King of the Hill" was the last TV show to portray "a straight white male patriarch" in a positive light.

He declared the widely accepted estimate that six million Jews died in the Holocaust "overblown." He said that while the Nazi leader Heinrich Himmler wanted to exterminate groups like Slavs and homosexuals, Hitler "was a lot more kind of chill on those subjects."

"I think he was a guy who really believed in his cause," he said of Hitler. "He really believed he was fighting for his people and doing what he thought was right."

He said he wanted to see the United States become "an actually fair, meritocratic society." Absent that, he would settle for a white ethnostate "where things are fair, because there's no competing demographics for government power or for resources."

His fascist ideal, he said, would resemble the early days in the United States, when power was reserved for landowners "and, you know, normies didn't really have a whole hell of a lot to say."

His faith in mainstream solutions slipped as he toured the country with one of the metal bands. "I got to see people who were genuinely

GEORGE ETHEREDGE FOR THE NEW YORK TIMES

"I don't want you to think I'm some 'edgy' Republican," Mr. Hovater said, while flatly denouncing the concept of democracy.

hurting," he said. "We played coast to coast, but specifically places in Appalachia, and a lot of the Eastern Seaboard had really been hurt."

### FRIENDSHIPS MADE AND LOST

In 2012, Mr. Hovater was incensed by the media coverage of the Trayvon Martin shooting, believing the story had been distorted to make a villain of George Zimmerman, the white man who shot the black teenager. By that time, he and Ms. Hovater had been dating for a year or two. She was a small-town girl who had fallen away from the Catholic Church ("It was just really boring"), and once considered herself liberal.

But in the aftermath of the shooting, Ms. Hovater found herself on social media "questioning the official story," taking Mr. Zimmerman's side and finding herself blocked by some of her friends. Today, she says, she and Mr. Hovater are "pretty lined up" politically.

As they let their views be known, friends left and friends stayed.

"His views are horrible and repugnant and hate-filled," said Ethan Reynolds, a Republican and city councilman in New Carlisle, Ohio, who said he had befriended Mr. Hovater without knowing his extremism. "He was an acquaintance I regret knowing."

Jake Nolan, a guitarist in one of the bands Mr. Hovater played in, stuck with him. "There are people who literally go around Sieg Heiling," he said. "Then you have the people who just want the right to be proud of their heritage" — people, he said, who are standing up against "what appears to be an increasingly anti-white America."

Mr. Hovater befriended Mr. Heimbach in February 2015 at the Conservative Political Action Conference. Mr. Heimbach, who two years earlier had founded a White Student Union at Towson University in Maryland, was holding a protest outside the proceedings and praising Vladimir Putin. The pair founded the Traditionalist Worker Party in the spring.

Soon Mr. Hovater was telling people that he would be running for a council seat in his hometown, New Carlisle, population 5,600. The announcement caught the attention of the Southern Poverty Law Center and the heavy metal press. But he never filed papers.

On a recent weekday evening, Mr. Hovater was at home, sautéing minced garlic with chili flakes and waiting for his pasta to boil. The cats were wandering in and out of their tidy little rental house. Books about Mussolini and Hitler shared shelf space with a stack of Nintendo Wii games. A day earlier, a next-door neighbor, whom Mr. Hovater doesn't know very well, had hung a Confederate flag in front of his house.

"This is kind of brackish territory here," Mr. Hovater said. "A lot of people consider Cincinnati the most northern Southern city."

The pasta was ready. Ms. Hovater talked about how frightening it was this summer to watch from home as the Charlottesville rally spun out of control. Mr. Hovater said he was glad the movement had grown.

They spoke about their future — about moving to a bigger place, about their honeymoon, about having kids.

# Free Speech and the Necessity of Discomfort

OPINION | BY BRET STEPHENS | FEB. 22, 2018

*This is the text of a lecture delivered at the University of Michigan on Tuesday. The speech was sponsored by Wallace House.*

I'D LIKE TO EXPRESS my appreciation for Lynette Clemetson and her team at Knight-Wallace for hosting me in Ann Arbor today. It's a great honor. I think of Knight-Wallace as a citadel of American journalism. And, Lord knows, we need a few citadels, because journalism today is a profession under several sieges.

To name a few:

There is the economic siege, particularly the collapse of traditional revenue streams, which has undermined the ability of scores of news organizations to remain financially healthy and invest in the kind of in-depth investigative, enterprise, local and foreign reporting this country so desperately needs.

There is a cultural siege, as exemplified by the fact that a growing number of Americans seem to think that if something is reported in the so-called mainstream media, it is *ipso facto* untrue.

There's a technological siege, which not only has changed the way we work, and distribute our work, but has also created a new ecosystem in which it is increasingly difficult to distinguish fact from opinion, clickbait from substance, and real news from fake.

Then — need I even mention it? — there is the president of the United States. We are all familiar with the ways in which Donald Trump's demagogic assault on the press has already normalized presidential mendacity, mainstreamed "alternative facts" and desensitized millions of Americans to both. I'll get to him in a moment.

But there is also a fifth siege, and this is the one I want to focus on today: This is the siege of the perpetually enraged part of our audience.

This is no small thing when it comes to the health, reputation and future prospects of our profession. Journalism, by its nature, must necessarily be responsive to its audience, attuned to its interests, sensible to its tastes, alert to its evolution. Fail to do this, and you might not survive as a news organization, never mind as an editor, reporter or columnist.

At the same time, journalism can only be *as good* as its audience. Intelligent coverage requires intelligent readers, viewers and listeners.

We cannot invest in long-form, in-depth journalism for readers interested only in headlines, first paragraphs, or list-icles. We cannot purchase the services of talented wordsmiths and expert editors if people are indifferent to the quality of prose. We cannot maintain expensive foreign bureaus if audiences are uninterested in the world beyond our shores. We cannot expect columnists to be provocative if readers cancel their subscriptions the moment they feel "triggered" by an opinion they dislike.

In sum, we cannot be the keepers of what you might call liberal civilization — I'm using the word liberal in its broad, philosophical sense, not the narrowly American ideological one — if our readers have illiberal instincts, incurious minds, short attention spans and even shorter fuses.

AN EXAMPLE: Last November, The New York Times published a profile of a 29-year-old Ohio man named Tony Hovater. Mr. Hovater is a welder from a suburb of Dayton. He's happily married, middle class, polite, plays drums, cooks pasta *aglio e olio*, and loves "Seinfeld."

He is also a proud and avowed Nazi sympathizer. He started out on the political left, moved over to the Ron Paul right, and ended up marching with the anti-Semitic white nationalists at Charlottesville. He doesn't believe six million Jews died in the Holocaust, and thinks Hitler was "kind of chill."

The profile, by Times reporter Richard Fausset, was a brilliant case study in Hannah Arendt's "banality of evil." Hovater is not a thug, even if his ideas are thuggish; not a monster, even if he takes inspiration from one; not insane, even if his ideas are crazy. He reminds us that a diabolical ideology gains strength not because devils propagate it, but because ordinary men embrace it. And he warns us, as Bertolt Brecht put it after the war, "The womb is fertile still, from which that crawled."

Lest anyone doubt what Fausset and his editors at the Times think of Hovater and his ideas, the article was titled "A Voice of Hate in America's Heartland." This is not, to say the least, a neutral way of introducing the subject.

Yet that did not seem enough for some Times readers, who erupted with fury at the publication of the article. Nate Silver, the Times's former polling guru, said the article did "more to normalize neo-Nazism than anything I've read in long time." An editor at The Washington Post accused us of producing "long, glowing profiles of Nazis" when we should have focused on the "victims of their ideologies." The Times followed up with an explanatory, and somewhat apologetic, note from the national editor.

No doubt, there may have been ways to improve the profile. There always are. But there was something disproportionate, not to say dismaying, about the way that so many readers rained scorn on The Times's good-faith effort to better understand just what it is that makes someone like Hovater tick.

Just what do these readers think a newspaper is supposed to do?

A NEWSPAPER, after all, isn't supposed to be a form of mental comfort food. We are not an advocacy group, a support network, a cheering section, or a church affirming a particular faith — except, that is, a faith in hard and relentless questioning. Our authority derives from our willingness to *challenge* authority, not only the authority of those in power, but also that of commonplace assumptions and conventional wisdom.

In other words, if we aren't making our readers uncomfortable every day, we aren't doing our job. There's an old saying that the role of the journalist is to afflict the comfortable and comfort the afflicted, but the saying is wrong. The role of the journalist is to afflict, period. News is *new* — new information, new challenges, new ideas — and it is meant to unsettle us.

That's a good thing. To be unsettled and discomforted is the world's great motivator. It is a prick to conscience, a prod to thinking, a rebuke to complacency and a spur to action.

Now, when I say we need to be making our readers uncomfortable, I don't mean we should gratuitously insult them if we can avoid it. But neither should we make an effort to play to their biases, or feed this or that political narrative, or dish the dirt solely on the people we love to hate, or avoid certain topics for fear of stirring readers' anger, even if it means a few canceled subscriptions. Especially in an age in which subscribers account for an ever-greater share of our revenue, publishers will have to be as bold in standing up to occasional, if usually empty, threats of mass cancellations for this or that article as they were in standing up to the demands of advertisers in a previous era.

What I mean by making readers uncomfortable is to offer the kind of news that takes aim at your own deeply held convictions and shibboleths. There are people on the political right who don't like hearing that the correlation between firearms and homicides is positive, not inverse — but a positive correlation is what the data show. Some environmentalists may believe that genetically modified "Frankenfoods" are bad for your health, but the overwhelming weight of scientific evidence tells us they are fine to eat.

The truth may set you free, but first it is going to tick you (or at least a lot of other people) off. This is why free speech requires constitutional protection, especially in a democratic society. Free speech may be the most essential vehicle for getting the truth out. But the truth, as anyone minimally versed in history knows, is rarely popular at first.

Barely 50 years ago, it was an unpopular truth that there was absolutely nothing unnatural about the love that went by the horrible name of "miscegenation." Other unpopular truths one could mention include gay rights, women's suffrage, and evolution. These truths could only have made their debut in the public square, and eventually gained broad acceptance, under the armed guard, so to speak, of the First Amendment.

But not just the First Amendment. In addition to a legal sanction, free speech has flourished in the United States because we have had a longstanding cultural bias in favor of the gadfly, the muckraker, the contrarian, the social nuisance. For over a century, editors and publishers and producers — at least the more enlightened ones — have gone out of their way to make allowances for opposing points of view.

They do so not because they have no strong convictions of their own, but rather out of a profound understanding that the astute presentation of divergent views makes us more thoughtful, not less; and that we cannot disagree intelligently unless we first understand profoundly. They do so because they believe that social progress depends on occasionally airing outrageous ideas that, on close reflection, aren't outrageous at all. They hold firm to the conviction that moving readers out of their political or moral comfort zones, even at the risk of causing upset, is good for mind and soul. Ultimately, they do so because we will not be able to preserve the culture and institutions of a liberal republic unless we are prepared to accept, as Judge Learned Hand put it in 1944, that the "spirit of liberty is the spirit which is not too sure that it is right" — and must therefore have the willingness to listen to the other side.

This was what Adolph Ochs knew in 1896, when he promised that under his stewardship The New York Times would "invite intelligent discussion from all shades of opinion." The Times, like other papers, may not have always lived up to that promise as well as it might have done. But as some of you may have noticed, it most emphatically is now, to the loud consternation of many of our readers.

I DO MY BEST to appreciate the concerns of these readers. I understand that many of them — many of *us* — believe the 2016 election marked a political watershed in which liberties we have long taken for granted are being attacked and possibly jeopardized by a president whose open contempt for a free press has few precedents in American history. I understand the justifiable fear these readers have for a White House in which the truth is merely optional, and in which normal standards of courtesy or decency have lost the purchase they previously had under Democratic and Republican administrations alike.

I also understand that these readers see The New York Times as a citadel, if not *the* citadel, in standing up to this relentless assault by the president and his minions. I think they are right. The country needs at least one great news organization that understands that the truth is neither relative nor illusory nor a function of the prevailing structure of power — but also that the truth is many-sided; that none of us has a lock on it; and that we can best approach it through the patient accumulation of facts and a vigorous and fair contest of ideas.

That, at any rate, is what I think we are trying to do at The Times, and I can only hope that more people will see its virtue as time goes by. That obviously demands good and consistent communication on our part. But, to return to my theme today, it also requires intelligence on the part of our readers.

How can we get our readers to understand that the purpose of The Times is not to be a tacit partner in the so-called Resistance, which would only validate the administration's charge that the paper is engaged in veiled partisanship rather than straight-up fact-finding and truth telling?

Some readers, for example, still resent The Times for some of the unflattering coverage of Hillary Clinton throughout the campaign, as if the paper's patriotic duty was to write fluff pieces about her in order to smooth her way to high office. Again, do these readers comprehend that we are in the business of news, not public relations? And does it not also occur to them that perhaps the real problem was coverage that was not aggressive *enough*, allowing Mrs. Clinton to dominate the Democratic field in 2016 despite her serious, and only belatedly apparent, shortcomings as a candidate?

As it is, it is not as if there is a great surfeit of pro-Trump news and opinion in the pages of The Times. I think that's a shortcoming of ours. We are a country in which about 40 percent of voters seem to be solidly behind the president, and it behooves us to understand and even empathize with them, rather than indulge in caricatures. Donald Trump became president because millions of Americans who voted for Barack Obama in 2012 voted Republican four years later. Those who claim this presidency is purely a product of racism need some better explanation to account for that remarkable switch.

THE DEEPER POINT, however, is that if one really wants to "resist" Trump, especially those of us in the news media, we might start by trying not to imitate him or behave the way he does.

The president is hostile to the First Amendment. Let's be consistent and expansive champions of the First Amendment. The president belittles and humiliates his political rivals. Let's listen to and respect our detractors. The president loves to feel insulted and indignant, because his skin is thin and it thrills his base. Let's hold off on the hair-trigger instinct to take offense. The president accuses first, gathers evidence later. Let's do the opposite. The president embraces ugly forms of white-identity politics. Let's eschew identity politics in general in favor of old-fashioned concepts of citizenship and universalism.

I could go on, but you get the point. The answer to a politics of right-wing illiberalism is not a politics of left-wing illiberalism. It is a politics of liberalism, period.

This is politics that believes in the virtues of openness, reason, toleration, dissent, second-guessing, respectful but robust debate, individual conscience and dignity, a sense of decency and also a sense of humor. In a word, Enlightenment. It's a capacious politics, with plenty of room for the editorials of, say, The New York Times and those of The Wall Street Journal. And it is an uncomfortable politics, because it requires that each side recognize the rights and legitimacy, and perhaps even the value, of the other.

THE NOMINATION AND ELECTION of Trump was, for me, the plainest evidence of the extent to which the liberal spirit has withered on the political right. I've written and spoken about this phenomenon many times before, so I won't get into it here. What worries me is the extent to which it is equally prevalent on the political left.

Case in point: Last month, I wrote a column under the title, "A Modest Immigration Proposal: Ban Jews."

The word "modest" might have been a tip-off to modestly educated readers that I was not, in fact, proposing to ban Jews at all. My point was to note that Jewish immigrants of a century ago, including my own ancestors, faced the same prejudices that modern-day immigrants from "S-hole" countries face today, and yet went on to great success. In other words, it was a pro-immigration piece, in line with the many other pro-immigration pieces I've written for the Times.

Social media went berserk. I was called a "literal Nazi," guilty of "garden variety bigotry." Others accused me of giving aid and comfort to neo-Nazis, even if I wasn't quite a neo-Nazi myself. A great deal of the reaction was abusive and obscene.

By now I'm sufficiently immunized to the way social media works that none of this hurts me personally, at least not too much. And, at its best, platforms such as Twitter are useful for injecting more speech, from a vastly wider and more diverse variety of voices than we ever heard from before, into our national conversation.

What bothers me is that too many people, including those who are supposed to be the gatekeepers of liberal culture, are using these platforms to try to shut down the speech of others, ruin their reputations, and publicly humiliate them.

How many people bother to read before they condemn? Are people genuinely offended, or are they looking for a pretext to be offended — because taking offense is now the shortest route to political empowerment? Am I, as a columnist, no longer allowed to use irony as a rhetorical device because there's always a risk that bigots and dimwits might take it the wrong way? Can I rely on context to make my point clear, or must I write in fear that any sentence can be ripped out of context and pasted on Twitter to be used against me? Is a plodding, Pravda-like earnestness of tone and substance the only safe way going forward?

Perhaps the most worrisome question is: To what extent are people censoring themselves for fear of arousing the social media frenzies? There's a reason why Katie Roiphe is writing about the "whisper networks" of women who aren't 100 percent in line with the #MeToo movement. It should profoundly alarm anyone who cares for #MeToo that such a piece should have needed to be written, in the reliably liberal pages of Harper's Magazine, no less. The job of #MeToo is to put a firm and hopefully final stop to every form of sexual predation, not to enforce speech codes.

This move toward left-wing illiberalism is not new, and the list of thinkers who have waged war against that illiberalism, from Arthur Schlesinger Jr. in the 1940s to Christopher Hitchens in the 2000s, amounts to a roll call of liberal honor. I think we are awaiting our new Hitchens today, in case any of you want to apply for the job. All you need is a first-class brain and a cast-iron stomach.

SO WHERE DOES this leave us?

I gave this talk the title: "Free Speech and the Necessity of Discomfort." Yesterday morning, when I retweeted Knight-Wallace's tweet advertising this speech, someone wrote, "Man, I hope he gets shouted down at some point." Maybe he was being ironic. At any rate, I'm happy to note that none of you has shouted me down — so far!

I trust that's because all of you recognize that, even if I may have said some things that made you uncomfortable and with which you profoundly disagree, there is a vast difference between intellectual challenge and verbal thuggishness, between a robust and productive exchange of ideas and mere bombast, between light and heat.

It's fair to say that Americans of different ideological stripes feel that many things have gone profoundly amiss in our social and political life in recent years. We all have our diagnoses as to what those things are. But one of them, surely, is that we are rapidly losing the ability to talk to one another.

The president has led the way in modeling this uncivil style of discourse. But he has plenty of imitators on the progressive left, who are equally eager to bully or shame their opponents into shutting up because they deem their ideas morally backward or insufficiently "woke." As each side gathers round in their respective echo chambers and social media silos, the purpose of free speech has become increasingly more obscure.

Its purpose isn't, or isn't merely, to allow us to hear our own voices, or the voices of those with whom we already agree. It is also to hear what other people, with other views, often anathema to ours, have to say.

To hear such speech may make us uncomfortable. As well it should. Discomfort is not injury. An intellectual provocation is not a physical assault. It's a stimulus. Over time, it can improve our own arguments, and sometimes even change our minds.

In either case, it's hard to see how we can't benefit from it, if we choose to do so. Make that choice. Democracy is enriched if you do. So are you.

**BRET STEPHENS** is an Op-Ed columnist at The New York TImes.

# What the Alt-Right Really Means

OPINION | BY CHRISTOPHER CALDWELL | DEC. 2, 2016

NOT EVEN THOSE most depressed about Donald J. Trump's election and what it might portend could have envisioned the scene that took place just before Thanksgiving in a meeting room a few blocks from the White House. The white nationalist Richard B. Spencer was rallying about 200 kindred spirits.

"We are not meant to live in shame and weakness and disgrace," he said. "We were not meant to beg for moral validation from some of the most despicable creatures to ever populate the planet." When Mr. Spencer shouted, "Hail, Trump! Hail, our people! Hail, victory!" a scattered half-dozen men stood and raised their arms in Nazi salutes.

Mr. Spencer, however you describe him, calls himself a part of the "alt-right" — a new term for an informal and ill-defined collection of

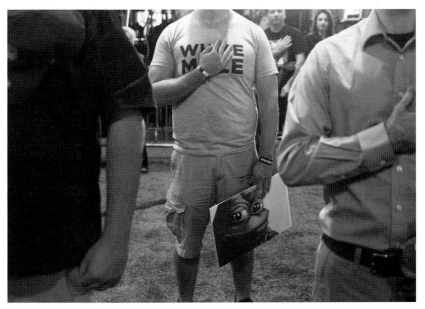

DAMON WINTER/THE NEW YORK TIMES

An attendee at a Trump campaign event in New Hampshire in September.

internet-based radicals. As such, he poses a complication for the incoming president. Stephen K. Bannon, the executive chairman of Breitbart News, whom Mr. Trump has picked as his chief White House strategist, told an interviewer in July that he considered Breitbart a "platform for the alt-right."

Perhaps we should not make too much of this. Mr. Bannon may have meant something quite different by the term. Last summer "alt-right," though it carried overtones of extremism, was not an outright synonym for ideologies like Mr. Spencer's. But in late August, Hillary Clinton devoted a speech to the alt-right, calling it simply a new label for an old kind of white supremacy that Mr. Trump was shamelessly exploiting.

Groups such as Mr. Spencer's, which had indeed rallied behind Mr. Trump, were delighted with the attention. Mr. Spencer called the days after the Clinton speech "maybe the greatest week we ever had." While he does not consider either Mr. Trump or Mr. Bannon alt-right, Mr. Spencer has expressed hope that the press's describing them as such will help his own group grow.

The alt-right is not a large movement, but the prominence that it is enjoying in the early days of the Trump era may tell us something about the way the country is changing. At least since the end of the Cold War, and certainly since the election of a black president in 2008, America's shifting identity — political, cultural and racial — has given rise to many questions about who we are as a nation. But one kind of answer was off the table: the suggestion that America's multicultural present might, in any way, be a comedown from its past had become a taboo. This year a candidate broke it. He promised to "make America great again." And he won the presidency.

Mr. Trump's success is bound to embolden other dissenters. This could mean a political climate in which reservations about such multi-culturalist policies as affirmative action are voiced more strenuously. It could mean a rise in racial conflict and a platform for alarming movements like Mr. Spencer's. More likely, it is going to bring a hard-to-interpret mix of those things.

Mr. Spencer, 38, directs the National Policy Institute, which sponsored the Washington meeting. Despite its name, the institute has little to say about policy, although it has called for a 50-year moratorium on immigration. What it mostly does is seek to unite people around the proposition that, as Mr. Spencer put it, "Race is real, race matters, and race is the foundation of identity."

There are many such groups, varying along a spectrum of couth and intellect. Mr. Spencer, who dropped out of a doctoral program at Duke and worked, briefly, as an editor for The American Conservative, has his own online review, Radix Journal. The eloquent Yale-educated author Jared Taylor, who hosts the American Renaissance website and magazine, was at the conference, too. Kevin MacDonald, a retired psychology professor whose trilogy on Jewish influence is a touchstone for the movement, also came. There were cheers from the crowd at the mention of Andrew Anglin, who runs a neo-Nazi website called The Daily Stormer, but he was not there. Neither was Greg Johnson, whose online review Counter-Currents translates right-wing writings from various European languages. Some of these groups sprouted on the internet. Others have been around since before it existed.

There is no obvious catchall word for them. The word "racist" has been stretched to cover an attitude toward biology, a disposition to hate, and a varying set of policy preferences, from stop-and-frisk policing to repatriating illegal immigrants. While everyone in this set of groups is racist in at least one of these senses, many are not racist in others. Not many of the attendees at the Washington gathering favored the term "white supremacist." The word implies a claim to superiority — something few insisted on. "White nationalist" is closer to the mark; most people in this part of the alt-right think whites either ought to have a nation or constitute one already. But they feel that almost all words tend to misdescribe or stigmatize them.

Almost all of them are gung-ho for Mr. Trump. That is a surprise. "I've been watching these people for 17 years," said Heidi Beirich, who follows extremist movements for the Southern Poverty Law Center. "It's the first time I've seen them come out for a candidate."

Mr. Trump disavowed the alt-righters once the excesses of Mr. Spencer's conference went viral. But as a candidate, Mr. Trump called the government corrupt, assailed the Republican establishment, flouted almost every rule of political etiquette, racial and otherwise, and did so in a way that made the alt-righters trust his instincts. And whether or not he exploited them as shamelessly as Mrs. Clinton alleged, he did little to put the public at ease on the matter — retweeting posts from someone called @WhiteGenocideTM and dawdling before disavowing the endorsement of the former Ku Klux Klan leader David Duke.

"I don't think that Trump is a rabid white nationalist," the alt-right blogger Millennial Woes said at a speech in Seattle days after the election. "I think that he just wants to restore America to what he knew as a young man, as a child. And I think he probably does know at some level that the way to do it is to get more white people here and fewer brown people."

Mr. Spencer speaks of Mr. Trump's campaign as a "body without a head" and considers many of his policies "half-baked." But for him, that is not the point. "Donald Trump is the first step towards identity politics for European-Americans in the United States," he said.

There is no good evidence that Mr. Trump or Mr. Bannon think in terms like these. Not even the former Breitbart editor at large Ben Shapiro, who has become an energetic critic of Mr. Bannon and his agenda, says that Mr. Bannon is himself a racist or an anti-Semite. Mr. Shapiro considers fears that Mr. Bannon will bring white nationalism to the White House "overstated, at the very least."

To be sure, Mr. Bannon holds right-wing views. He believes that a "global Tea Party movement" is underway, one that would fight crony capitalism and defend Western culture against radical Islam. In a 2014 speech he showed an interest in linking up American activists with certain European populist movements, including opponents of both the European Union and same-sex marriage. But while he recognized that some groups, such as France's National Front, had "baggage, both ethnically and racially," he expressed confidence that their intolerance "will all be worked through with time."

Until Hillary Clinton's speech last summer, a similarly broad idea prevailed of what the alt-right was. The Southern Poverty Law Center's webpage on the movement traces some of its roots to libertarian followers of Ron Paul and traditionalist Christians. Neither were in evidence at the National Policy Institute conference in Washington. The adjective "alt-right" has been attached in the past to those, like the undercover documentarian James O'Keefe (known for his secret recordings of Planned Parenthood encounters), whose conservatism is mainstream, even if their tactics are not. Understood this way, the alt-right did look as if it might be a pillar of Mr. Bannon's world Tea Party.

This was especially so if you worked for one of Mr. Bannon's enterprises. Last March, Breitbart's Milo Yiannopoulos, a peroxide-blond gay Trump supporter, critic of feminism and internet "troll" of a particularly aggressive kind, helped write "An Establishment Conservative's Guide to the Alt-Right," which painted the movement as "born out of the youthful, subversive, underground edges of the internet," treating the neo-Nazis in its ranks as unrepresentative.

But since then, and certainly since the National Policy Institute event, alt-right has come more and more to mean white nationalist. Mr. Yiannopoulos's exuberant youths look peripheral to the movement, the extremists central. William Johnson of the American Freedom Party even wrote Mr. Spencer a letter accusing him of squandering what might have been a "start-over moniker" — a gentler term that didn't invite immediate dismissal — for his fellow white nationalists.

How big is the movement? There is a "hard core" of thousands or tens of thousands who are "taking us seriously on a daily basis," Mr. Spencer said. But both members and detractors have an incentive to exaggerate the alt-right's size. The National Policy Institute, at this point, would have trouble holding a serious street rally, let alone turning into a mass political party.

Even so, this more narrowly defined alt-right may be a force. In the internet age, political consciousness can be raised not just through quarterlies, parties and rallies but also through comment boards, console games and music videos. The internet solves the organizing problem of mobs, even as it gives them incentives not to stray from their screens. The adjective "alt-right" does not just denote recycled extremist views — it also reflects the way those views have been pollinated by other internet concerns and updated in the process.

For example, the alt-right has an environmentalist component, centered on a neo-pagan group called the Wolves of Vinland. The Norwegian heavy-metal musician Varg Vikernes, after serving 16 years for murder, has an alt-right blog that contains his musings on everything from Norse mythology to the meaning of the Norwegian mass murderer Anders Breivik. There are sci-fi and video-game enthusiasts, too, including many who participated in the "GamerGate" uproar of 2014, which pitted (as the alt-right sees it) feminist game designers trying to emasculate the gaming world against (as the feminists saw it) a bunch of misogynist losers.

But most of all there is sex. The alt-right has a lot of young men in it, young men whose ideology can be assumed to confront them with obstacles to meeting people and dating. Sex-cynicism and race-pessimism, of course, often travel in tandem. At the National Policy Institute conference, the writer F. Roger Devlin gave a talk on why young Norwegian women in Groruddalen, outside Oslo, preferred dating Somali and Pakistani gang members to ethnic Norwegian boys-next-door. "The female instinct is to mate with socially dominant men," he explained, "and it does not matter how such dominance is achieved."

Likewise, the common alt-right slur "cuckservative," a portmanteau combining cuckold and conservative, is not just a colorful way of saying that establishment conservatives have been unmanly.

According to Matthew Tait, a young ex-member of the far-right British National Party, the metaphor has a precise ornithological meaning. Like the reed-warbler hatching eggs that a cuckoo (from which the word "cuckold" comes) has dropped into its nest, cuckservatives are raising the offspring of their foes. One can apply the metaphor equally to progressive ideas or to the children of the foreign-born. Type "reed warbler" into YouTube, and you will find a video with more than a million views, along with a considerable thread of alt-right commentary.

The internet liberates us to be our worst selves. Where other movements have orators and activists, the alt-right also has ruthless trolls and "doxers." The trolls bombard Twitter and email accounts with slur-filled letters and Photoshopped art. Doxing is the releasing of personal information onto the internet. Last month, several alt-right writers, including Mr. Spencer, had their accounts suspended by Twitter. Mr. Spencer says he appreciates the "frenetic energy" of trolling but doesn't do it himself.

The alt-right did not invent these tactics. But during this election the trolling reached a sadistic pitch. Journalists who opposed Mr. Trump received photos of themselves — and in some cases their children — dead, or in gas chambers. Jewish and Jewish-surnamed journalists were particular targets, especially those seen to be thwarting Mr. Trump's rise: Jonah Goldberg, Julia Ioffe and Ben Shapiro, among others. The Daily Stormer has been particularly aggressive in deploying its "troll army" against those with whom it disagrees. A signature punctuation of the alt-right is to mark Jewish names with "echoes," or triple parentheses, like (((this))).

One got a strange sensation at the National Policy Institute gathering that everyone in the room was either over 60 or under 40. There was a lot of tomorrow-belongs-to-me optimism, as if the attendees felt the ideas being aired there were on the verge of going mainstream. Whether this had anything to do with Mr. Trump's victory or the effect of alt-right rebranding was hard for a newcomer to say. As Mr. Spencer spoke, a dapper guy named Ryan looked on. Ryan was a

27-year-old who sported the common "fashy" haircut — close-cropped (like a skinhead) on the sides, free-flowing (like a mullet) on the top. Mr. Spencer was lecturing journalists about how it took courage to embrace a movement that was "quite frankly, heretical."

"For the moment," Ryan muttered.

Mr. Tait, who hopes to start an alt-right movement in England, said: "What you're seeing now is young people who have never been affiliated to any kind of politics, ever. They don't remember what it was like before the war or in the 1960s or even in the 1980s. Their motivation isn't a sense of loss." That is what is "alt" about the alt-right. These people are not nostalgic. They may not even be conservatives. For them, multiculturalism is not an affront to traditional notions of society, as it would have been in the Reagan era. It is society.

The Vanderbilt University political scientist Carol Swain was among the first to describe the contours of this worldview. In her 2002 book, "The New White Nationalism in America," she noted that young people were quick to identify double standards, and that they sometimes did so in the name of legitimate policy concerns. "I knew that identity would come next," she recalled. "It had to come. All they had to do was copy what they were hearing. The multiculturalist arguments you hear on every campus — those work for whites, too." Mr. Spencer, asked in an interview how he would respond to the accusation that his group was practicing identity politics in the manner of blacks and Hispanics, replied: "I'd say: 'Yuh. You're right.' "

Professor Swain's analysis does not just pertain to radicals. It is a plausible account of what is happening in the American electoral mainstream. The alt-right is small. It may remain so. And yet, while small, it is part of something this election showed to be much bigger: the emergence of white people, who evidently feel their identity is under attack, as a "minority"-style political bloc.

CHRISTOPHER CALDWELL, a senior editor at The Weekly Standard, is at work on a book about the rise and fall of the post-1960s political order.

# Behind 2016's Turmoil,
# a Crisis of White Identity

BY AMANDA TAUB | NOV. 1, 2016

CALL IT the crisis of whiteness.

White anxiety has fueled this year's political tumult in the West: Britain's surprising vote to exit the European Union, Donald J. Trump's unexpected capture of the Republican presidential nomination in the United States, the rise of right-wing nationalism in Norway, Hungary, Austria and Greece.

Whiteness, in this context, is more than just skin color. You could define it as membership in the "ethno-national majority," but that's a mouthful. What it really means is the privilege of not being defined as "other."

ERIC THAYER FOR THE NEW YORK TIMES

Supporters of Donald J. Trump, the Republican presidential nominee, during a rally last month in Naples, Fla.

Whiteness means being part of the group whose appearance, traditions, religion and even food are the default norm. It's being a person who, by unspoken rules, was long entitled as part of "us" instead of "them."

But national and racial identity were often conflated for the white majority. That identity felt to many white people like one of the most important pillars holding up their world — and now it seems under threat.

There are, of course, complicated contours to 2016's unusual politics. In Britain, immigrants from South Asia voted heavily to leave the European Union, citing hopes that curtailing European migration might open space for more people from Asia. In the United States, frustration with and alienation from status quo politics have helped drive Mr. Trump's rise.

There has also always been a certain fluidity to this concept of whiteness. Irish and Italian immigrants to the United States, and Jews in Britain, were once seen as separate from the white national majority, and are now generally considered part of it, benefiting from racial privilege. At the same time, Jews' white skin did not protect them from being cast as outsiders by some of Mr. Trump's supporters who have circulated anti-Semitic memes on social media.

Still, experts see a crisis of white identity underlying much of the West's current turmoil.

"It's fundamentally about 'who are we?' " said Eric Kaufmann, a professor of politics at Birkbeck College, University of London. "What does it mean to be part of this nation? Is it not 'our' nation anymore, 'our' meaning the ethnic majority?

"These kinds of questions are really front and center, even though they're not necessarily verbalized."

The questions can seem like a sudden reversal after decades of rising multiculturalism, through the civil rights movement in the United States and the European Union's opening up of borders.

In fact, academic research suggests that other economic and social transformations unfolding at the same time have led many people to

A "Leave" rally in London in June, before Britain's referendum on European Union membership.

anchor themselves more fully in their whiteness — even as whiteness itself has lost currency.

"When I look at the data, I keep coming back to this issue that it's really about identity politics," said Elisabeth Ivarsflaten, a professor at Norway's University of Bergen who studies Europe's far-right parties. "This is the most powerful predictor of support for the populists."

### GAINS AND LOSSES IN A CHANGING WORLD

Identity, as academics define it, falls into two broad categories: "achieved" identity derived from personal effort, and "ascribed" identity based on innate characteristics.

Everyone has both, but people tend to be most attached to their "best" identity — the one that offers the most social status or privileges. Successful professionals, for example, often define their identities primarily through their careers.

For generations, working-class whites were doubly blessed: They enjoyed privileged status based on race, as well as the fruits of broad economic growth.

White people's officially privileged status waned over the latter half of the 20th century with the demise of discriminatory practices in, say, university admissions. But rising wages, an expanding social safety net and new educational opportunities helped offset that. Most white adults were wealthier and more successful than their parents, and confident that their children would do better still.

That feeling of success may have provided a sort of identity in itself.

But as Western manufacturing and industry have declined, taking many working-class towns with them, parents and grandparents have found that the opportunities they once had are unavailable to the next generation.

That creates an identity vacuum to be filled.

"For someone who is lower income or lower class," Professor Kaufmann explained, "you're going to get more self-esteem out of a communal identity such as ethnicity or the nation than you would out of any sort of achieved identity."

Focusing on lost identities rather than lost livelihoods helps answer one of the most puzzling questions about the link between economic stress and the rise of nationalist politics: why it is flowing from the middle and working classes, and not the very poor.

While globalization and free trade have widened economic inequality and deeply wounded many working-class communities, data suggests that this year's political turmoil is not merely a backlash to that real pain.

In Britain's referendum on membership in the European Union, low education was a much stronger predictor of people voting "leave" than low income, according to an analysis by Zsolt Darvas, a senior fellow at the Bruegel research group.

A recent Gallup study found that Mr. Trump's supporters tend to earn above-average incomes for their communities, but also tend to live in majority-white areas where children are likely to be worse off

Supporters took photos with their phones as Mr. Trump arrived for a rally last month in Sanford, Fla.

than their parents. Arlie Russell Hochschild, the author of "Strangers in Their Own Land: Anger and Mourning on the American Right," describes a feeling of lost opportunity as the "deep story" of the rural Louisiana communities she spent four years studying.

Her subjects felt like they were waiting in a long line to reach the top of a hill where the American dream was waiting for them. But the line's uphill progress had slowed, even stopped. And immigrants, black people and other "outsiders" seemed to be cutting the line.

For many Western whites, opportunities for achieved identity — the top of the hill — seem unattainable. So their ascribed identity — their whiteness — feels more important than ever.

## WHITENESS IS BECOMING LESS VALUABLE

Michael Ignatieff, a historian and former Liberal Party leader in

Canada, said that in much of the West, "what defined the political community" for many years "was the unstated premise that it was white." The formal rejection of racial discrimination in those societies has, by extension, constructed a new, broader national identity. The United States has a black president; London has a Muslim mayor of Pakistani descent.

But that broadening can, to some, feel like a painful loss, articulated in the demand voiced over and over at Trump rallies, pro-Brexit events and gatherings for populist parties throughout Europe: "I want my country back."

The mantra is not all about bigotry. Rather, being part of a culture designed around people's own community and customs is a constant background hum of reassurance, of belonging.

The loss of that comforting hum has accelerated a phenomenon that Robin DiAngelo, a lecturer and author, calls "white fragility" — the stress white people feel when they confront the knowledge that they are neither special nor the default; that whiteness is just a race like any other.

Fragility leads to feelings of insecurity, defensiveness, even threat. And it can trigger a backlash against those who are perceived as outsiders.

Even some conservative analysts who support a multiethnic "melting pot" national identity, such as the editor of National Review, Reihan Salam, worry that unassimilated immigrants could threaten core national values and cultural cohesion.

### THE EFFECT OF RAPID CHANGE

Social scientists, after crunching data from both sides of the Atlantic, have discovered something surprising: It's not the amount of racial or ethnic diversity in a community that predicts white resentment and support of anti-immigrant policies, but the pace of change.

Denmark, for instance, is 88 percent white Danish today — hardly a majority in jeopardy. But a generation ago, in 1980, it was

A rally for Mr. Trump in Tampa, Fla. Experts see a crisis of white identity underlying much of the West's current turmoil.

97 percent white. The anti-immigrant Danish People's Party is now the second-largest party in the Danish Parliament. In Germany, where the foreign-born population shot up by approximately 75 percent between 2011 and 2015, the anti-immigrant, populist Alternative for Germany party is now drawing record support.

Britain saw a 66 percent increase in its foreign-born population between 2004 and 2014. Voters who chose "leave" in the recent referendum overwhelmingly cited immigration as their main concern.

Professor Kaufmann and a colleague, Gareth Harris, found that white Britons who lived in areas that are rapidly diversifying became more likely to vote for the right-wing British National Party. Daniel Hopkins, a professor of political science at the University of Pennsylvania, found a similar pattern of ethnic change leading to anti-immigrant politics in the United States.

Immigrant populations in Arkansas, North Carolina and Tennessee have more than tripled since 1990, noted Lee Drutman, a senior fellow at the New America Foundation, in an analysis for Vox. Anxiety over those changes may explain why the Republican Party became so much more focused on limiting immigration over that period — and why white voters in those states overwhelmingly support Mr. Trump.

## THE WHITENESS TABOO

For decades, the language of white identity has only existed in the context of white supremacy. When that became taboo, it left white identity politics without a vocabulary.

If you are a working-class white person and you fear that the new, cosmopolitan world will destroy or diminish an identity you cherish, you have no culturally acceptable way to articulate what you perceive as a crisis.

Some of these people have instead reached for issues that feel close to their concerns: trade, crime, the war on drugs, controlling the borders, fear of Islamist terrorism. All are significant in their own right, and create very real fears for many people, but they have also become a means to have a public conversation about what society's changes mean for white majorities.

Professor Ivarsflaten cited the U.K. Independence Party, whose official platform focused on Brexit but whose pitch to voters emphasized immigrants' effects on the economy and culture, as an example of an effective hybrid populist pitch.

The approach has in some cases moved from the political fringes into the mainstream. Some leaders from Britain's center-right, governing Conservative Party, for example, helped push a British exit, and since the referendum the new Conservative prime minister, Theresa May, has signaled sympathy with white identity politics.

Mrs. May's government proposed a rule that would publicly shame employers who hired foreign workers. And her first major speech was full of barbs directed against multiculturalism, including a jab against people who claimed to be "citizens of the world," whom she called "citizens of nowhere."

But the struggle for white identity is not just a political problem; it is about the "deep story" of feeling stuck while others move forward.

There will not likely be a return to the whiteness of social dominance and exclusive national identity. Immigration cannot be halted without damaging Western nations' economies; immigrants who have already arrived cannot be expelled en masse without causing social and moral damage. And the other groups who seem to be "cutting in line" are in fact getting a chance at progress that was long denied them.

Western whites have a place within their nations' new, broader national identities. But unless they accept it, the crisis of whiteness seems likely to continue.

**AMANDA TAUB** writes The Interpreter column for The New York Times.

# The Pull of Racial Patronage

OPINION | BY ROSS DOUTHAT | AUG. 17, 2016

THINK OF A Donald Trump voter, the kind that various studies have identified as his archetypal backer: a white man without a college education living in a region experiencing economic distress.

What do you see? A new "forgotten man," ignored by elites in both parties, suffering through socioeconomic dislocations, and turning to Trump because he seems willing to put the working class first? Or a resentful white bigot, lashing back against the transformation of America by rallying around a candidate who promises to make America safe for racism once again?

You're allowed to answer "both, depending." But where to lay the emphasis has divided liberals and conservatives against one another.

HILARY SWIFT FOR THE NEW YORK TIMES

Donald J. Trump supporters in Fairfield, Conn., last Saturday.

Conservatives who are generally happy with the Republican Party's status quo, the mix of policies that Trump has ranged himself against, have stressed his voters' baser proclivities and passions, dismissing them as bigots who are really the authors of their own unhappy fates.

Conservatives who favor a populist shift in how the G.O.P. approaches issues like taxes or transfer programs have stressed the ways in which Reaganite Republicanism has failed the working class, while urging a conservative politics of solidarity that borrows at least something from the wreck of Trumpism.

Likewise on the left: The more content you are with a liberalism in which social issues provide most of the Democratic Party's energy, the more likely you'll be to crack wise on Twitter — "a lot of economic anxiety here!" — every time Trump or one of his hangers-on or supporters makes a xenophobic foray.

Alternatively, the more you favor a left-wing politics that stresses economic forces above all else, the more you'll cast Trump's blue collar support as the bitter fruit of the Democratic Party's turn to neoliberalism, and argue that social democracy rather than shaming and shunning is the cure for right-wing populism.

My sympathies are with the second group in both debates — as a partisan of a more solidaristic conservatism, and as an outsider who prefers the old left's class politics to the pseudo-cosmopolitanism of elite liberalism today.

But it's also important for partisans of socioeconomic solidarity, whether right wing or left wing, to recognize that racial and economic grievances can't always be separated, and that a politics of ethnic competition is an unfortunately common state of political affairs.

Consider the trajectory of liberalism. In the 1930s, Franklin Roosevelt's New Deal deliberately excluded blacks from certain benefits and job programs. This was discrimination, but it was also patronage: It was a time when "affirmative action was white," to borrow from the historian Ira Katznelson, lifting white workers at the expense of African-Americans.

Then decades later, liberalism moved to create affirmative action programs to help those same African-Americans. This was redress and expiation, but it was also another form of patronage: a promise of a hand up, a race-based advantage that only liberalism would provide.

With time, that promise was extended to groups with weaker claims to redress than the descendants of American slaves, even as mass immigration expanded the potential pool of beneficiaries. Eventually, we ended up with a liberalism that favors permanent preferences for minority groups, permanently large immigration flows — plus welfare programs that recent immigrants are more likely than native-born Americans to use.

This combination is (mostly) rooted in idealism. But it still amounts to a system of ethnic patronage, which white Americans who are neither well-off nor poor enough to be on Medicaid see as particularly biased against them.

This constituency, the gainfully employed but insecure lower middle class, is the Trumpian core. By embracing white identity politics, they're being bigoted but also, in their own eyes, imitative: Trump's protectionist argle-bargle boils down to a desire to once again have policies that specifically benefit lower-middle-class whites — welfare for legacy industries and affirmative action for white men.

This crude attempt at imitation, unfortunately, is part of a very common iterative cycle in politics. It's a reason why, in multiethnic societies, multiracial parties are the exception rather than the rule.

And breaking that cycle won't be easy for either party. The activist energy on the left is pushing for a more ethnically focused politics, devoted to righting structural race-based wrongs. That energy will be blunted temporarily by the flight of well-educated whites from Trump, but the absence of economic common ground between Hillary-voting white moderates and the party's poorer, minority base means that her temporary coalition is likely to fracture first along racial lines.

That fracturing will help the G.O.P. recover, but it won't help Republicans build a pan-racial conservatism. The pull of white identity politics can be overcome, but only with great effort. Not least because it requires not only that conservatism change, but that minority voters be persuaded that the change is meaningful.

And after Trump, what forgiveness?

**ROSS DOUTHAT** is an Op-Ed columnist for The New York Times.

# Why Trump Supporters Distrust Immigration and Diversity

OPINION | BY FREDERICK R. LYNCH | AUG. 4, 2017

PRESIDENT TRUMP'S SUPPORT for a proposal from Senators Tom Cotton and David Perdue that slashes legal immigration and reports about the Justice Department's renewed interests in scrutinizing college affirmative action programs should come as no surprise. Mr. Trump is catering to his largely middle-aged, white, middle- and working-class base. That's what politicians do.

But is he addressing legitimate interest-group concerns or is he pandering to racial fears? There is a rather one-sided debate over what motivates Mr. Trump and his supporters. A wave of new books and articles still invoke stereotypes trotted out on election night: Mr. Trump's "angry white voters" were motivated by racism, resentment,

DOUG MILLS/THE NEW YORK TIMES

The audience for an address by President Trump in Huntington, W.Va., on Thursday.

"whitelash," declining economic or social status, irrational fears of economic or demographic change, or all of the above. They are deluded, confused "Strangers in Their Own Land," as suggested by the title of a book by the sociologist Arlie Hochschild.

This thinly veiled scorn has inhibited deeper study of whether Mr. Trump's white voters are responding to legitimate economic threats generated by what I have termed "the diversity machine." This powerful policy juggernaut has quietly and questionably blended together two trends that threaten working- and middle-class whites.

First, high levels of legal and illegal immigration, as the Harvard economist George Borjas's recent book emphasizes, have produced wage losses among some poor and working-class low-skilled native-born workers. Wealthy whites and corporations were often the winners. It's the old story of costs and benefits of building America on the backs of cheap immigrant labor.

For more than a hundred years, these split labor markets have often pitted native-born workers (mostly white, sometimes unionized) against successive waves of cheap-labor newcomers (usually of different ethnicity or culture or both). Economic competition fuels ethnic antagonism — and nativism, racism and the like.

There has been very little scholarly or public attention paid to a second policy trend that intensified the antagonism born of this ethnically split labor market. In the 1990s, affirmative action's original mission to right past wrongs against African-Americans was transformed into an expanded list of preferences in the workplace and in higher education for immigrant subgroups (for example, Hispanics, Asians or Pacific Islanders).

Instead of redressing past discrimination, the more ambitious diversity mission was to achieve proportional, "look like America" institutions that allegedly would perform better by reflecting the country's demographic change. Preferences for blacks were controversial, but even critics had to admit that they had some degree of historical and moral authority. Not so the expansion of preferences to members of ill-defined, grab-bag racial and ethnic categories. (For example, "Hispanic" could include first-through-fourth-generation Americans of Cuban, Mexican, Guatemalan, Bolivian, Chilean, Salvadoran, Colombian and other Latin American ancestry.)

The system of expanding diversity preferences and much immigration policy have often been formulated and imposed by bureaucrats and judges. But in several states, voters approved ballot measures like Michigan's Proposition 2 banning ethnic preferences, or legislatures passed laws placing controls on illegal immigration (the latter, such as Arizona's Senate Bill 1070, sometimes undone, in part or in whole, by the courts).

A 2016 Gallup poll on affirmative action was typical in finding majorities of all groups (76 percent of whites) who believed that merit alone should determine college admissions, with race or ethnicity playing a relatively minor role. Nevertheless, just last year, a closely divided Supreme Court affirmed an earlier decision that narrow use of race may be one of the many factors in undergraduate admissions at the University of Texas.

There is good reason to suspect that universities may not follow the letter of the law. Data from the Association of American Medical Colleges indicate that race is a substantial factor in medical school admissions, not one of many. For example, from 2013 to 2016, medical schools in the United States accepted 94 percent of blacks, 83 percent of Hispanics, 63 percent of whites and 58 percent of Asians with top MCAT scores of 30 to 32 and grade-point averages of 3.6 to 3.8; for MCAT scores of 27 to 29 (G.P.A. of 3.4 to 3.6), the corresponding figures are 81 percent, 60 percent, 29 percent and 21 percent. For low-range MCAT scores of 24-26 (G.P.A. of 3.2 to 3.4), 57 percent of blacks were admitted, 31 percent of Hispanics, 8 percent of whites and 6 percent of Asians.

The presidential candidates in 2016 were largely silent on affirmative action, but Mr. Trump said in 2015 that he was "fine with it" though "it's coming to a time when maybe we don't need it." Affirmative action and new diversity dictates were most likely an "unspoken but heard" issue.

Institutional racism remains a problem, as does immigration and the balancing of assimilation and pluralism. But identity politics and identity policies may have become too divisive and complicated in both theory and practice.

Since the election, many Democrats have been talking less about diversity and more about unifying cultural and economic common-alities. The new Democratic "Better Deal" populist blueprint put forward by Senator Charles Schumer of New York echoes his admi-ration for the New Deal by emphasizing strategies that would help all American workers.

Mr. Schumer knows his party must quickly and candidly address the question of why the white working and middle classes — groups who were the foundation of Franklin Roosevelt's New Deal coalition — often support Mr. Trump.

**FREDERICK R. LYNCH** is a government professor at Claremont McKenna College and the author of "The Diversity Machine: The Drive to Change the 'White Male Workplace.'"

# We're All Fascists Now

OPINION | BY BARI WEISS | MARCH 7, 2018

CHRISTINA HOFF SOMMERS is a self-identified feminist and registered Democrat with a Ph.D. in philosophy and a wicked sense of humor. She is also a woman who says bad things. Things like: Men and women are equal, but there are differences between them. Or: The gender gap in STEM fields isn't simply the result of sexism. Or: Contrary to received wisdom, the American school system actually favors girls, not boys.

When such a person steps foot on a college campus these days, you know what's coming. So it was on Monday at Lewis & Clark Law School in Portland, Ore., where Ms. Sommers had been invited by the Federalist Society to give a talk about feminism.

In advance of the lecture, nine student groups, among them the Portland National Lawyers Guild, the Minority Law Student Association, the Women's Law Caucus, the Jewish Law Society and the school's Young Democratic Socialists of America chapter sent a letter protesting the appearance by this "known fascist."

The letter added that her invitation amounted to an "act of aggression and violence" and went on to offer a curious definition of free speech: "Freedom of speech is certainly an important tenet to a free, healthy society, but that freedom stops when it has a negative and violent impact on other individuals."

Yes, these future lawyers believe that free speech is acceptable only when it doesn't offend them. Which is to say, they don't believe in it at all.

For the lecture itself, a student wearing a jacket emblazoned with the command "Stay Woke" led protesters in shouting "Microaggressions are real" and "No platform for fascists." Ms. Sommers handled matters as gracefully as possible, but had delivered only half her lecture before Janet Steverson, a law professor and the school's dean of diversity and inclusion, asked her to cut her remarks short and take questions from the hardy souls who somehow survived the violence of her words.

At this point, such incidents have become so routine that it's tempting to wave them off.

We shouldn't. What happened to Ms. Sommers on Monday is a telling example of a wider phenomenon that reaches well beyond the confines of campus. Call it the moral flattening of the earth.

We live in a world in which politically fascistic behavior, if not the actual philosophy, is unquestionably on the rise. Italy just gave the plurality of its vote to a party that is highly sympathetic to Vladimir Putin. The Philippines is in the grip of a homicidal maniac who is allying himself with Xi Jinping. Mr. Xi just anointed himself president for life and has banned the words "Animal Farm" and "disagree" from Chinese internet searches. Bashar al-Assad is winning in Syria, where half a million people have so far been slaughtered. Dictatorship and starvation have descended on Venezuela. At its annual conference in Washington last month, the Conservative Political Action Committee gave its stage, and its enthusiastic applause, to a member of France's National Front. That's just a short list.

Yet these are generally not the extremists that leftists focus on. Instead, they seem to believe that the real cause for concern are the secret authoritarians passing as liberals and conservatives in our midst.

Among them:

Laura Kipnis, a feminist film-studies professor at Northwestern who wrote an essay for The Chronicle of Higher Education about how there are too many Title IX sexual misconduct investigations on campuses — and then had two graduate students file a Title IX complaint against her, on the grounds that her article created a "hostile environment."

Or Ayaan Hirsi Ali, a Somali-born former Muslim and feminist who the Southern Poverty Law Center insists is in fact a "propagandist" who is "far outside the political mainstream."

Or Mary Beard, the celebrated Cambridge classicist and self-described "bloody lefty" who recently published a book-length manifesto denouncing the world's long history of misogyny. Last month, Ms. Beard commented on a scandal gripping Britain: Oxfam workers in Haiti after the 2010 earthquake are accused of hiring prostitutes, including, reportedly, underage girls. "Of course one can't condone the (alleged) behavior of Oxfam staff in Haiti and elsewhere," she wrote. "But I do wonder how hard it must be to sustain 'civilized' values in a disaster zone."

For expressing the thought that people in lawless places often behave in terrible ways, Ms. Beard was torn apart on social media as an "absolute monster" who was somehow excusing the exploitation of vulnerable women and girls. Her Cambridge colleague, Priyamvada Gopal joined in, accusing her of "patrician white 'feminist' racism."

Why are so many demonstrably non-fascist people being accused of fascism?

Partly, this phenomenon is driven by our current political moment, in which millions of Americans — and not just those who identify as liberals or progressives — are horrified by the policies and the rhetoric oozing out of the White House. When the shadow of genuine chaos and extremism looms, people tend to get jumpy.

Partly, as the writer David French and others have pointed out, this ritual we keep witnessing of an in-group wielding its power against a perceived heretic seems to come from a deep human desire for a sense of belonging and purpose. Organized religion may be anathema on the political left, but the need for the things religion provides — moral fervor, meaning, a sense of community — are not.

Partly, too, it is the result of a lack of political proportion and priority. It's instructive that students at the University of Chicago spent their energy a few years back protesting Dan Savage, the progressive sex columnist who used the word "tranny" in a talk that included a discussion about reclaiming words, while ignoring a lecture the very same week by former Senator Rick Santorum, the Pennsylvania Republican who has compared gay relationships to bestiality. Freud called this the narcissism of small differences.

But it is also a concerted attempt to significantly redraw the bounds of acceptable thought and speech. By tossing people like Mary Beard and Christina Hoff Sommers into the slop bucket with the likes of Richard Spencer, they are attempting to place their reasonable ideas firmly outside the mainstream. They are trying to make criticism of identity politics, radical Islam and third-wave feminism, among various other subjects, verboten. For even the most minor transgressions, as in the case of Professor Beard, people are turned radioactive.

There are consequences to all this "fascism" — and not just the reputational damage to those who are smeared, though there is surely that.

The main effect is that these endless accusations of "fascism" or "misogyny" or "alt-right" dull the effects of the words themselves. As they are stripped of meaning, they strip us of our sharpness — of our ability to react forcefully to real fascists and misogynists or members of the alt-right.

For a case study in how this numbing of the political senses works, look no further than Mitt Romney and John McCain. They were roundly denounced as right-wing extremists. Then Donald Trump came along and the words meant to warn us against him had already been rendered hollow.

Orwell warned that the English language "becomes ugly and inaccurate because our thoughts are foolish, but the slovenliness of our language makes it easier for us to have foolish thoughts." He added, however, that "the process is reversible."

Will true liberals do what it takes to reverse it? We can only hope so, because the battle against genuine authoritarian threats needs to be waged consistently, credibly and persuasively. For that to happen, words need to mean something. Calling women like Christina Hoff Sommers and Mary Beard fascists and racists only helps the other side.

**BARI WEISS** is a staff editor and writer for the Opinion section.

# A Renaissance on the Right

OPINION | BY DAVID BROOKS | APRIL 12, 2018

WHAT'S BAD FOR THE GAVEL is good for the pen. The Republican Party is in the midst of a cataclysmic transformation. But all the political turmoil is creating a burst of intellectual creativity on the right.

Young, fresh writers are bursting on the scene: Sohrab Ahmari, Helen Andrews, Charles Cooke, Mollie Hemingway, Jason Willick, Michael Brendan Dougherty, Gracy Olmstead, James Poulos, Oren Cass, Matthew Schmitz and many others.

Suddenly fundamental issues, like the values of the liberal democratic order itself, are up for debate. Some conservatives are laying down comprehensive critiques of the way our society is organized. Modern liberal capitalism is too soulless, they say, too atomizing, too destructive of basic institutions like family, faith and village that give life meaning. Liberal individualism doesn't produce the sort of virtuous, self-restrained people that are required to sustain it.

Other conservatives are rising to defend that order, including National Review's Jonah Goldberg, who later this month comes out with his epic and debate-shifting book, "Suicide of the West."

Goldberg points out that for eons human beings were semi-hairless upright apes clumped in tribes and fighting for food. But about 300 years ago something that he calls "the Miracle" happened. It was a shift in attitude. For thousands of years, societies divided people into permanent categories of race or caste. But, Goldberg writes, "the Miracle ushered in a philosophy that says each person is to be judged and respected on account of their own merits, not the class or caste of their ancestors."

That belief, championed by John Locke, or a story we tell about Locke, paved the way for human equality, pluralism, democracy, capitalism and the idea that a person can have a plurality of identities and a society can contain a plurality of moral creeds.

It also proved to be the goose that laid the golden egg. Economic growth exploded. The American founding asserted that Lockean ideas are universal. And nothing had ever succeeded like America. Between 1860 and 1900 alone, America's population doubled and its wealth grew fivefold.

But we have stopped teaching about the Miracle, Goldberg says, and stopped feeling grateful for it.

Tribalism was always there, lurking under the surface. It returns now as identity politics, which is reactionary reversion to the pre-modern world. Identity politics takes individual merit out of the moral center of our system and asserts that group is, Goldberg says, "an immutable category, a permanent tribe." Identity politics warriors claim they are fighting for social justice, but really it's just the same old thing, Goldberg argues, a mass mobilization to gain power for the tribe.

Earlier movements wanted America to live up to its ideals. Today's identitarians doubt the liberal project itself.

Identity politics gained traction on the left, but now the Trumpian right has decided to fight fire with fire. Populism is a form of identity politics because it's based on in-group/out-group distinctions. It says anybody who doesn't think or look like us is not a true American.

This tribal mentality is tearing the civic fabric and creates a war of what Goldberg thinks of as "ecstatic schadenfreude" — the exaltation people feel when tribal foes are brought down.

I love the way Goldberg provocatively tells his story, but I partially disagree with it. The central tension in his book is between Locke, who emerges as a rational, calm, pipe-smoking economist, and Jean-Jacques Rousseau, who emerges as a wild-haired, passionately resentful rock star. The liberal order emerges from the individualism of Locke and is threatened by group consciousness and romantic resentments of Rousseau.

But America is both rational and romantic, both Locke and Rousseau. We have a rationalist constitution, but we have a shared national faith and are an emotional community, rooted in our land, inspired by our history, warmed by the hope of our common future.

The core problem today is not tribalism. It's excessive individualism, which has eaten away at our uniting faith and damaged our relationships with one another. Excessive individualism has left us distrustful and alone — naked Lockeans. When people are naked and alone they revert to tribe. Tribalism is the end product of excessive individualism.

Goldberg is suspicious of nationalism and has a tendency to think that any effort to build a national community puts you on the express lanes on the road to serfdom.

His conservatism is missing the bonding sentiments of Edmund Burke, and the idea that the little platoon of the family is nestled in the emotional platoon of the neighborhood and the emotional platoon of the nation. Tribalism is not the only way to form a group; there's also the redeeming and forgiving love of community, and a shared national faith. Goldberg misses the way Hamilton, Lincoln and Theodore Roosevelt built a national community that didn't crush local communities but rather reinforced them.

Goldberg is right to fight tribalism on the left and the right. But you can't reweave a fragmented nation by appealing just to Lockean individualism. Gratitude is too weak a glue to hold a diverse nation together. Renewal will come through the communitarians on the right and the left, who seek ways to improve relationships on a household, local and national level.

**DAVID BROOKS** is an Op-Ed columnist for The New York Times.

# Liberal Blind Spots Are Hiding the Truth About 'Trump Country'

OPINION | BY SARAH SMARSH | JULY 19, 2018

*For one thing, it's not Trump country. Most struggling whites I know here live a life of quiet desperation, mad at their white bosses, not resentful toward their co-workers or neighbors of color.*

WICHITA, KAN. — Is the white working class an angry, backward monolith — some 90 million white Americans without college degrees, all standing around in factories and fields thumping their dirty hands with baseball bats? You might think so after two years of media fixation on this version of the aggrieved laborer: male, Caucasian, conservative, racist, sexist.

This account does white supremacy a great service in several ways: It ignores workers of color, along with humane, even progressive white workers. It allows college-educated white liberals to signal superior virtue while denying the sins of their own place and class. And it conceals well-informed, formally educated white conservatives — from middle-class suburbia to the highest ranks of influence — who voted for Donald Trump in legions.

The trouble begins with language: Elite pundits regularly misuse "working class" as shorthand for right-wing white guys wearing tool belts. My father, a white man and lifelong construction worker who labors alongside immigrants and people of color on job sites across the Midwest and South working for a Kansas-based general contractor owned by a woman, would never make such an error.

Most struggling whites I know live lives of quiet desperation mad at their white bosses, not resentment of their co-workers or neighbors of color. My dad's previous three bosses were all white men he loathed for abuses of privilege and people.

It is unfair power that my father despises. The last rant I heard him on was not about race or immigration but about the recent royal wedding, the spectacle of which made him sick.

"What's so special about the royals?" he told me over the phone from a cheap motel after work. "But they'll get the best health care, the best education, the best food. Meanwhile I'm in Marion, Arkansas. All I want is some chickens and a garden and place to go fishing once in a while."

What my father seeks is not a return to times that were worse for women and people of color but progress toward a society in which everyone can get by, including his white, college-educated son who graduated into the Great Recession and for 10 years sold his own plasma for gas money. After being laid off during that recession in 2008, my dad had to cash in his retirement to make ends meet while looking for another job. He has labored nearly every day of his life and has no savings beyond Social Security.

Yes, my father is angry at someone. But it is not his co-worker Gem, a Filipino immigrant with whom he has split a room to pocket some of the per diem from their employer, or Francisco, a Hispanic crew member with whom he recently built a Wendy's north of Memphis. His anger, rather, is directed at bosses who exploit labor and governments that punish the working poor — two sides of a capitalist democracy that bleeds people like him dry.

"Corporations," Dad said. "That's it. That's the point of the sword that's killing us."

Among white workers, this negative energy has been manipulated to great political effect by a conservative trifecta in media, private interest and celebrity that we might call Fox, Koch and Trump.

As my dad told me, "There's jackasses on every level of the food chain — but those jackasses are the ones that play all these other jackasses."

Still, millions of white working-class people have refused to be played. They have resisted the traps of racism, sexism, homophobia, xenophobia and nationalism and voted the other way — or, in too many cases, not voted at all. I am far less interested in calls for empathy toward struggling white Americans who spout or abide hatred than I am in tapping into the political power of those who don't.

Like many Midwestern workers I know, my dad has more in common ideologically with New York's Democratic Socialist congressional candidate Alexandria Ocasio-Cortez than with the white Republicans who run our state. Having spent most of his life doing dangerous, underpaid work without health insurance, he supports the ideas of single-payer health care and a universal basic income.

Much has been made of the white working class's political shift to the right. But Mr. Trump won among white college graduates, too. According to those same exit polls trotted out to blame the "uneducated," 49 percent of whites with degrees picked Mr. Trump, while 45 percent picked Hillary Clinton (among them, support for Mr. Trump was stronger among men). Such Americans hardly "vote against their own best interest." Media coverage suggests that economically distressed whiteness elected Mr. Trump, when in fact it was just plain whiteness.

Stories dispelling the persistent notion that bigotry is the sole province of "uneducated" people in derided "flyover" states are right before our eyes: A white man caught on camera assaulting a black man at a white-supremacist rally last August in Charlottesville, Va., was recently identified as a California engineer. This year, a white male lawyer berated restaurant workers for speaking Spanish in New York City. A white, female, Stanford-educated chemical engineer called the Oakland, Calif., police on a family for, it would appear, barbecuing while black.

Among the 30 states tidily declared "red" after the 2016 election, in two-thirds of them Mrs. Clinton received 35 to 48 percent of the vote. My white working-class family was part of that large minority, rendered invisible by the Electoral College and graphics that paint each state red or blue.

In the meantime, critical stories here in "red states" go underdiscussed and underreported, including:

**Barriers to voting.** Forces more influential than the political leanings of a white factory worker decide election outcomes: gerrymandering, super PACs, corrupt officials. In Kansas, Secretary of State Kris Kobach blocked 30,000 would-be voters from casting ballots (and was recently held in contempt of federal court for doing so).

**Different information sources.** Some of my political views shifted when my location, peer group and news sources changed during my college years. Many Americans today have a glut of information but poor media literacy — hard to rectify if you work on your feet all day, don't own a computer and didn't get a chance to learn the vocabulary of national discourse.

**Populism on the left.** Today, "populism" is often used interchangeably with "far right." But the American left is experiencing a populist boom. According to its national director, Democratic Socialists of America nearly quadrupled in size from 2016 to 2017 — and saw its biggest one-day boost the day after Ms. Ocasio-Cortez's recent primary upset. Progressive congressional candidates with working-class backgrounds and platforms have major support heading into the midterms here in Kansas, including the white civil rights attorney James Thompson, who grew up in poverty, and Sharice Davids, a Native American lawyer who would be the first openly lesbian representative from Kansas.

To find a more accurate vision of these United States, we must resist pat narratives about any group — including the working class on whom our current political situation is most often pinned. The greatest con of 2016 was not persuading a white laborer to vote for a nasty billionaire with soft hands. Rather, it was persuading a watchdog press to cast every working-class American in the same mold. The resulting national conversation, which seeks to rename my home "Trump Country," elevates a white supremacist agenda by undermining resistance and solidarity where it is most urgent and brave.

SARAH SMARSH (@Sarah_Smarsh) is the author of the forthcoming "Heartland: A Memoir of Working Hard and Being Broke in the Richest Country on Earth."

# Feminism and LGBTQ Rights

In many ways, feminism evolved as a part of identity politics — and, along with the civil rights movement, the wom-
en's rights movement has provided the greatest successes
for marginalized peoples under the guise of identity politics
in the United States. More recently, as contemporary
societies have come to understand the spectrum of gender
and sexual identities a person might have, LGBTQ rights
have also been in focus. While some political rights have
finally been granted to members of the LGBTQ community
in the United States, the range and role of identity politics
remains hotly debated within the community itself.

## When Hillary Clinton Killed Feminism

OPINION | BY MAUREEN DOWD | FEB. 14, 2016

WASHINGTON — The Clinton campaign is shellshocked over the whole-
sale rejection of Hillary by young women, younger versions of herself
who do not relate to her.

Hillary's coronation was predicated on a conviction that has
just gone up in smoke. The Clintons felt that Barack Obama had
presumptuously snatched what was rightfully hers in 2008, gliding
past her with his pretty words to make history before she could.

So this time, the Clintons assumed, the women who had deserted
Hillary for Barack, in Congress and in the country, owed her. Democrats would want to knock down that second barrier.

Hillary believed that there was an implicit understanding with the sisters of the world that now was the time to come back home and vote for a woman. (The Clintons seem to have conveniently forgotten how outraged they were by identity politics when black leaders deserted them in 2008 to support Obama.)

This attitude intensified the unappetizing solipsistic subtext of her campaign, which is "What is Hillary owed?" It turned out that female voters seem to be looking at Hillary as a candidate rather than as a historical imperative. And she's coming up drastically short on trustworthiness.

As Olivia Sauer, an 18-year-old college freshman who caucused for Bernie Sanders in Ames, Iowa, told a Times reporter: "It seems like he is at the point in his life when he is really saying what he is thinking. With Hillary, sometimes you get this feeling that all of her sentences are owned by someone."

Hillary started, both last time and this, from a place of entitlement,

Young women at a Bernie Sanders rally in Nashua, N.H., on Monday.

as though if she reads her résumé long enough people will surrender. And now she's even angrier that she has been shown up by someone she considers even less qualified than Obama was when he usurped her place.

Bernie has a clear, concise "we" message, even if it's pie-in-the-sky: The game is rigged and we have to take the country back from the privileged few and make it work for everyone. Hillary has an "I" message: I have been abused and misunderstood and it's my turn.

It's a victim mind-set that is exhausting, especially because the Clintons' messes are of their own making.

On the trail in New Hampshire, Madeleine Albright made the case that it was a betrayal of feminist ideals to support Bernie against Hillary, noting that "there's a special place in hell for women who don't help each other." When Sanders handily won the women's vote on Tuesday, David Axelrod noted dryly that they were going to need to clear out a lot of space in hell.

And in a misstep for the feminist leader who got famous by going undercover as a Playboy bunny, Gloria Steinem told Bill Maher that young women were flocking to Bernie to be where the boys are. Blaming it on hormones was odd, given the fact that for centuries, it was widely believed that women's biology made them emotionally unfit to be leaders.

What the three older women seemed to miss was that the young women supporting Sanders are living the feminist dream, where gender no longer restricts and defines your choices, where girls grow up knowing they can be anything they want. The aspirations of '70s feminism are now baked into the culture.

The interesting thing about the spectacle of older women trying to shame younger ones on behalf of Hillary is that Hillary and Bill killed the integrity of institutional feminism back in the '90s — with the help of Albright and Steinem.

Instead of just admitting that he had had an affair with Monica Lewinsky and taking his lumps, Bill lied and hid behind the skirts of his wife and female cabinet members, who had to go out before the cameras and vouch for his veracity, even when it was apparent he was lying.

Seeing Albright, the first female secretary of state, give cover to President Clinton was a low point in women's rights. As was the New York Times op-ed by Steinem, arguing that Lewinsky's will was not violated, so no feminist principles were violated. What about Clinton humiliating his wife and daughter and female cabinet members? What about a president taking advantage of a gargantuan power imbalance with a 22-year-old intern? What about imperiling his party with reckless behavior that put their feminist agenda at risk?

It rang hollow after the Anita Hill-Clarence Thomas hearings. When it was politically beneficial, the feminists went after Thomas for bad behavior and painted Hill as a victim. And later, when it was politically beneficial, they defended Bill's bad behavior and stayed mute as Clinton allies mauled his dalliances as trailer trash and stalkers.

The same feminists who were outraged at the portrayal of Hill by David Brock — then a Clinton foe but now bizarrely head of one of her "super PACs" — as "a little bit nutty and a little bit slutty," hypocritically went along when Hillary and other defenders of Bill used that same aspersion against Lewinsky.

Hillary knew that she could count on the complicity of feminist leaders and Democratic women in Congress who liked Bill's progressive policies on women. And that's always the ugly Faustian bargain with the Clintons, not only on the sex cover-ups but the money grabs: You can have our bright public service side as long as you accept our dark sketchy side.

Young women today, though, are playing by a different set of rules. And they don't like the Clintons setting themselves above the rules.

**MAUREEN DOWD** is an Op-Ed columnist for The New York Times.

# 'Bro'-liferation

ESSAY | BY WESLEY MORRIS | MARCH 15, 2016

ARE YOU A young or youngish man who prefers the company of other men? Platonically, platonically. (For the most part.) Are you currently wearing — or have you ever worn — baggy shorts? A baseball cap? A polo shirt? White sneakers? Sunglasses on your head? All at the same time? Are you white? And these other men whose company you enjoy, do you guys drink and watch sports together? Are they white, too? Have you been to see Mumford and Sons with them? What about Diplo? Or A$AP Rocky? If the New England Patriots tight end Rob Gronkowski announced that he was having a three-day party on a cruise ship, would you go?

Answering yes to even some of this — *Are you a youngish man?* — might make you a bro. And I'm sad for you. You didn't ask for this. Or maybe you did. Maybe you use the word "bro" as a form of address. As in: "Hey, bro." Or: "I can't tonight, bro." Or: "Derivatives are off the chain right now, bro." So you at least know of the concept of "the bro" and that a culture — of excessive devotion, of "bros before hos," of springbreak4ever — exists around your lifestyle.

But we're not talking about you, bro. Not right now. Now we're talking about the sort of bro who instigates the hijacking of Hillary Clinton's official Facebook page; who harasses women who endorse Clinton; who tells black Americans whom he thinks it's in their best interest to support. Yeah, we're talking about the Berniebro. I know: him, that Bernie Sanders supporter so badly feeling the Bern that he communicates in condescension and flames.

Indeed, "Berniebro," a term fancifully coined by Robinson Meyer in The Atlantic, became a catchall for a certain kind of dog-whistling, sexist proselytizing on Sanders's behalf, sometimes from his own staff. Jeff Weaver, Sanders's campaign manager, could have been auditioning for "Veep" when, last October, he said jokingly of

Clinton to John Heilemann of Bloomberg Politics that "we're willing to consider her for vice president. We'll give her serious consideration. We'll even interview her." Weaver's willingness "to consider her" was of a piece with a commentariat that is comfortable accusing Clinton and her supporters of a vulgar identity politics — or misogyny, even — for discussing Clinton's sex in the context of the presidency.

The deployment of "bro" as a means of disparagement is part of a generalized expression of fatigue with the wielding of white-male power, a feeling that has emboldened Clinton supporters. We're no longer talking about the classic bro. We're talking about trolls and, in lieu of a less printable word, jerks.

Classic bro adventure still exists. Rob Gronkowski, for instance, really did have that party. Last month, he summoned 700 people, at their own expense, for a weekend cruise — Gronk's Party Ship — from Miami to the Bahamas. The entertainment included Redfoo of LMFAO and Flo Rida, which, to bros, is like having Chewbacca and R2-D2 show up at your "Star Wars"-themed bar mitzvah. The Party Ship's website encouraged attendees to bring "your babes and your bros." And during the weekend, as Flo Rida and his band played "G.D.F.R.," Gronkowski, wearing sunglasses and a pair of shorts in two tones of an aquatic blue-green, humped the stage, turned his back to the crowd, bent his legs and wagged his butt as though it were attached to a jackhammer. (He twerked, basically.)

This was the bro, optimally: feeling good in front of an audience, without rhythm, shame or a shirt. This was the bro, suboptimally, too: Gronk's presumption that his fun is fun for everybody else. The Party Ship featured a version of the bro that America got to know on MTV's friends-at-the-beach reality sitcom, "Jersey Shore," which, to the consternation of Italian-Americans, Garden Staters and many sentient humans, ran from 2009 to 2012. The men on that show made such prolific use of the word that it occasionally abutted the palindromic, as in, "Bro, I'm telling you, bro."

Courtesy of "Jersey Shore," the bro became evidence of ridiculous male friendship, like the bond among veterans, but with self-tanner instead of casualties of war. The prominence of "bro" also coincided with the arrival of the joshing fraternal comedies of Judd Apatow and the cresting popularity of Barney Stinson, the sleazy, slutty suit Neil Patrick Harris played for nine seasons on "How I Met Your Mother," who adhered to the articles of a handbook called the Bro Code.

But now "bro" has been ripped from its life as a teasing term of endearment and description of camaraderie and plunked into the sociopolitical swamps of entitlement and privilege. It starts to get at the fractious identity rifts at the heart of this campaign season. On one hand, women and people of color don't want to be patronized by know-it-all white guys or bullied into supporting one presidential candidate and harassed away from supporting another. On the other: #NotAllMen.

What are white guys who just want to chill with one another supposed to do? Keep their mouths shut and legs closed, for starters. Jesting aside, though, that's the frustration fueling the current presidential election. White men are being called out for the transgressions of the last year and also, less obviously, for the lingering affronts of centuries past. (You know what they say: A fight about the dishes in the sink is about everything but the dishes.) Bruised male ids are running against rule-bound superegos. The irony is rich. It's also real: Bros be feelin' oppressed, yo!

It's also odd that "bro" has become a culturally white designation. The word has roots both in the church and as a way that black people address black men — as "brother." Black use of that word is publicly fraternal and privately political. It's how black men salute each other — still — in white spaces, as a way of saying to each other, "I see you." What's vaguely obnoxious about "bro" is that it doesn't really see anybody.

The willful blindness sometimes feels like a stab at utopia. White men calling black men "bro" aspire to or assume a kinship with black Americans. There are other words — O.K., the N-word — that the bro knows he can't say. "Brother" seemed O.K. Eventually, so did "bro." But I've heard more than one black man say, "Dude, I'm not your bro." I've been that man. There are regional variations on the word "bro" that seem designed to lock out certain white people: In the South, for instance, there's "bruh" and, in Hawaii and the American West, "brah." But a bro can always get a key made.

"Bro" draws a line between cultural blackness and cultural whiteness while also drawing a circle around white male groups. Its swell gets at a kind of vague discomfort we have with male camaraderie, even though certain comrade cohorts — like the dudes in "Entourage" or at Donald Trump events — invite derision. The bro, in all his permutations, can work the nerves. But the trawl used to fish him out seems indiscriminate, netting all senses of fraternity.

Where does the expanded taxonomy leave earnest, sensitive male bonds? American neologists coined a cheeky answer: bromance. Meanwhile, dudes who prefer doing everything with and just like other dudes (minus sex) are bromosexuals. And dudes who prefer the company of (and actual sex with) "masculine" guys are gaybros.

"Bro"-liferation presents an unhappy paradox. We're out of ideas for how to think about male behavior. And yet, lately certain male behavior has been so reliably hegemonic, so boorish, so violently intolerant that it needs to be classified, rounded up and put on notice. "Bro" puts a dunce cap on patriarchy.

**WESLEY MORRIS** is the critic at large for The New York Times and a contributing writer for the magazine.

# How Two Producers of 'Transparent' Made Their Own Trans Lives More Visible

BY EMILY BOBROW | SEPT. 13, 2016

IN A HOT NIGHT in July at Skylight Books in Los Angeles, Zackary Drucker and Rhys Ernst perched on stools to discuss their new book of photographs, "Relationship." It is by far the most personal of the many projects they have worked on together. The photographs chronicle their six-year romance, which ended soon after many of these images were shown at the Whitney Biennial in 2014.

Drucker and Ernst, who are perhaps better known as producers of the Emmy-winning Amazon series "Transparent," speak regularly about their work. But Drucker is plainly more at ease in the spotlight. She is tall and blond, with eyes as blue as swimming pools. That night she wore a white shift and high-heeled sling-backs, and she kept the microphone in its stand so she could gesture with her hands. The images, she told the audience, were meant as a private visual diary. "There was never an intent to show the photographs, even though we are both art-makers."

They are both 33 and around the same height, but Ernst appears slighter. Wearing light brown pants, bright white Reeboks and a diamond stud in his right ear, he explained that he and Drucker have backgrounds in "auto-ethnography," which he defined as "the practice of creating self-reflexive work, or work that reflected my community." This, he said, was a guiding impulse for the photographs in "Relationship."

Anyone familiar with the rush of young love will recognize its hallmarks in these photos: all smoldering looks, parted lips and bare limbs on rumpled sheets. Drucker and Ernst have an easy sexual charisma, but that's not what makes this series novel, even daring. During the years they were together, from 2008 to 2014, Drucker was in the process of transitioning from male to female, and Ernst from female to male. They met soon after they each began taking hormones, so the photographs also capture what Ernst has described as "the unflattering throes of yet another puberty." In calling this series "Relationship," Drucker and Ernst are describing not only their partnership but also their relationship with themselves and their genders, their choices and their bodies.

Though Drucker and Ernst are no longer a couple, they chose to publish these photographs anyway, because even as transgender stories are becoming more mainstream, there are few public examples of trans people leading ordinary lives, filled with love and lazy mornings. There are even fewer cases, as Drucker and Ernst emphasized that night in July, of trans people taking control over how they are represented.

On "Transparent," whose third season begins this month, their goal has been to ensure not just that trans people are depicted accurately on screen, but also that they are working behind the scenes — as writers, directors and personal assistants. Except for the character of Maura, a father who comes out to his family as trans, played by Jeffrey Tambor, every trans role on the show is filled by a trans person. The desire to see more transgender people in front of and behind the camera also informs much of Drucker's and Ernst's work as artists. Drucker is often the star of her own experimental videos and performances, which challenge conventional views of sex and gender. Her work has been shown at MoMA's PS1, the Museum of Contemporary Art in Chicago and SFMoMA. Ernst's narrative filmmaking tends to feature trans actors and documentary subjects and travel the film-festival circuit. He is at work on his first full-length feature, which he describes as a "middle-aged trans-guy buddy-movie comedy."

"I remember when we were installing the photographs at the Whitney, someone asked us: 'Oh, this is great. Who was the photographer?'" Ernst told the bookstore crowd. "They assumed we were just the subjects, which is of course the history of this kind of work. But this is what I hope changes going forward. It's the work we're doing in television. It's the work we're doing in filmmaking. It's the work we're doing in photography. It's making trans people the author, rather than just the subject. That's really the key."

POP-CULTURAL REPRESENTATIONS of trans people have historically reduced them to objects of pity or scorn. "Over and over again, somebody is crying in the mirror, taking off their wig," Ernst said over dinner at a gastropub near the Silver Lake home he shares with his partner, Patrick Staff, an artist. "There are these fixations that cis-gender people get that are not the way our lives are being lived at all." (To be "cis-gender" is to identify as the gender you are assigned at birth; i.e., not trans.) A prime example, he said, is "Dallas Buyers Club," a critically acclaimed film that earned Jared Leto an Oscar in 2014 for his supporting role as Rayon, an H.I.V.-positive trans woman. "She was a throwaway character," Ernst griped, "a drug addict who was there to make the protagonist learn about himself, and she was named after a synthetic fabric. That's not a real person."

In the two years since, there has been a marked political and cultural shift, and a growing public fascination with trans people. For Drucker and Ernst, whose work has always been about making the trans experience more visible, this has meant a much bigger audience. "There needs to be a little demystifying about trans existence," Ernst said. "That's why people have so many burning questions about it all."

Soon after their photographs were installed at the Whitney, they began working on the first season of "Transparent" with Jill Soloway, the show's creator. Soloway met Ernst when they each had a short film screening at the Sundance Film Festival in 2012. Soloway's father had just come out as trans, and she found herself opening up to Ernst about what she was going through. They kept in touch. After Soloway finished writing the "Transparent" pilot, she reached out to Ernst and Drucker, knowing that she needed trans people involved from the start. "Everyone knows and loves them," she told me in her office on the Paramount lot. "They're the homecoming king and queen of the trans movement."

Drucker and Ernst say the show has been able to "undo a lot of damage" when it comes to popular portrayals of trans people. Maura is not a sad loner whose every act and thought is about transitioning. Rather, she is the parent of a flawed but loving family in which everyone seems uncomfortable in their skin. Initially hired as consultants to prevent the show from trafficking in trans stereotypes, Drucker and Ernst were swiftly promoted to producers. They now offer notes on scripts, watch rough cuts of episodes and work closely with the writers and actors to make the trans performances as authentic as possible. Drucker helps Tambor understand how Maura feels about herself and her body, and she tweaks his mannerisms onscreen, regularly nudging him to close his legs, for example. Ernst directs the opening credits. Both also lead what they call "Trans 101" for everyone involved with the show, from Amazon executives to truck drivers, in which they explain the etiquette of working with trans colleagues. They stress that it is best to ask what pronoun people prefer. They advise against inquiring about the genitals or birth names of trans people, or referring to them as "trannies" or "she-males." "People are afraid of saying the wrong thing, so they don't have the conversation," Drucker says. "But I think there's no undignified questions, only undignified answers."

For many of the show's trans performers and crew members, all of this has been life-changing. "'Transparent' was my coming-out party," Trace Lysette said at the show's panel at Outfest, the L.G.B.T. film festival in Los Angeles, in July. Like many trans women, Lysette struggled for years to find employment, making money by stripping and sex work before she landed a recurring role as Shea, a friend of Maura's. "It's allowed me to get up off the pole and have a career that I never thought would really happen," she said. Silas Howard, the show's first trans director, says the call from Soloway was like getting "a golden ticket." Tambor has begun teaching acting classes for trans people in Los Angeles.

Drian Juarez, the program manager of the Transgender Economic Empowerment Project, a Los Angeles nonprofit group, told me that the show's success has inspired other companies, including NBC and Ryan Seacrest Productions, to ask her for leads on transgender talent for trans-related stories. Given that trans people are twice as likely to be unemployed as the general population (four times as likely if they are not white), these industry jobs are a big deal. Drucker and Ernst also persuaded Amazon to sponsor the Trans Pride festival in Los Angeles.

"I've just never seen any production like the familial, politi-cized, life-changing, worldview-changing empathy machine that is 'Transparent,'" Ernst told me. The show, he conceded, doesn't exactly represent a new norm in the industry, but he and Drucker hope that the many trans people involved in its production are gaining the tools necessary to make their own shows. "It's certainly the beginning of something new," Drucker says.

For the moment, working on "Transparent" has turned Drucker and Ernst into trans spokespeople in Hollywood. Drucker was among the trans women hired to help Caitlyn Jenner navigate her new trans life on the two-season E! Network series "I Am Cait." Focus Fea-tures asked Ernst to be a consultant on "The Danish Girl," a 2015 biopic about Lili Elbe, one of the first people to undergo gender-reassignment surgery. Ernst was wary, as the film was already underway with a cis-gender writer, director and star. Yet he found the studio receptive to his many recommendations, including his request that Focus "give back to the trans community in tangible ways." The studio created a $10,000 scholarship for trans filmmakers and helped fund a web series of documentary shorts about trans pio-neers called "We've Been Around," directed by Ernst, which had its premiere online in March. "Being trans right now necessitates this multihyphenate way of being," Drucker says.

WHEN DRUCKER AND Ernst were growing up in the 1990s, mass media presented trans people mainly on talk shows like "Jerry Springer," which tended to sensationalize with big reveals like "My Boyfriend Is a Girl!" and "Guess What ... I'm a Man!" "You knew you didn't want to be that, but at least there was something to point to," Drucker said. We were eating homemade tabbouleh at her house in Cypress Park, which she shares with her boyfriend of nearly two years, Jerid Bartow, an urban designer.

Finding models for how to live, or even a language to describe their feelings, was difficult for Drucker and Ernst. After Drucker discovered that she desired boys and Ernst that he liked girls (at least initially), they didn't feel right calling themselves gay or lesbian because it didn't feel as if they were attracted to the same sex. They were both relieved as teenagers to discover the term "queer," which is elastic enough to elide standard definitions of sexual orientation and gender.

Each was raised in a supportive home by compassionate parents — a rare privilege, they acknowledge. But public bathrooms were always sites of dread, and school was hard. Drucker's taste for blue hair, dog collars and makeup made her a target in Syracuse, her hometown. "She hid a lot from us," her mother, Penny Sori, told me. "It was only when I started working at the high school that I saw she took a lot of crap." When Drucker insisted on wearing a gown to the prom, her parents worried that she was putting herself at risk. But when Sori approached her, "Zackary looked at me in this funny way and said, 'I need your support on this.' So I said, 'O.K., let me find my long black gloves and at least accessorize you effectively.' "

Ernst was similarly ostracized and bullied in Chapel Hill, where his father, Carl Ernst, is an Islamic-studies professor at the University of North Carolina. As the only queer kid at his public middle school and later at the local Quaker school, he says, he was treated poorly by both students and teachers. With his parents' blessing, he dropped out in ninth grade. He studied art and music at home, set up a darkroom in his closet and took classes at local community colleges.

Art allowed them to vent their anger and defy convention. At her home, Drucker showed me a box of old photographs. Amid the pictures of her bar mitzvah ("a rare moment of gender conformity"), punk adolescence and androgynous college years was a series of snapshots from when she was 3 or 4, dressed in her mother's clothes and beaming. "Those photographs provided an opportunity for me to see myself outside of the constraints of my reality," she said. "Art-making has always provided this place to invent and reinvent myself."

Drucker went on to study photography at the School of Visual Arts in New York. Soon after arriving in the city in 2001, she met Flawless Sabrina, a revered drag performer otherwise known as Jack Doroshow, and the first of many "trans-feminine elders" Drucker collected in search of "proof that it's possible to have a sustainable life and live outside the rules." At Hampshire College, Ernst fell in love with mixed-media filmmaking, which allowed him to combine his many interests. For "The Drive North," a Super-8 short that Ernst made and starred in as a 20-year-old undergraduate, he used his own animation and original score and experimented with slide projections and energetic editing to tell a story about two teenagers driving to college. It earned him several prizes at festivals around the world. After graduation he moved to New York, where he began working as a personal assistant on film and television projects and eventually became a producer and editor on MTV.

Transitioning is a complicated and often stressful process. It took a while before it felt like a necessary step for either of them. Drucker always knew she flouted traditional gender categories, but she was able to maintain a level of androgyny until her early 20s. It was only when her body started aging in a masculine way that she realized "that wasn't the path I wanted to go down." After she moved to Los Angeles to attend the California Institute of the Arts in 2005, she began taking estrogen.

Although Ernst knew he wasn't female, transitioning made him nervous, particularly because he knew few people who had done it.

"It was still this kind of distant, weird relative of 'gay and lesbian,' and people didn't understand it," he says. Without public examples of happy, successful, aging trans people, he remembered wondering: Do people grow old? Do the hormones kill you? As a feminist, he asked himself: Do I even want to be a man?

He was also troubled by the fact that it is impossible to transition quietly. It feels extremely public, he explains, because essentially everyone else has to transition, too. "At what point would my mom change pronouns to her hairdresser when they chat about me? It really ripples. It feels like jumping off a cliff."

Ernst began taking hormones six months before driving cross-country with a trans-male friend to study filmmaking at CalArts. They were just starting to pass as men, which meant they were "dealing with the panopticon of rest-stop men's rooms for the first time." The experience was nerve-racking, but he learned that men don't really look at one another in men's rooms. He also found that people were much kinder to him than when he was a gender-nonconforming woman. "I got the, you know, 'Sup, chief? 'Sup, champ? It was really striking."

Drucker met Ernst at a party soon after he arrived in Los Angeles. "It was such a revelation when we got together," Drucker told me. Within a year they were subletting the rundown house of Ron Athey, a performance artist and mentor (they call him "Pops"). They collaborated on several projects, including "She Gone Rogue," a dreamy experimental short featuring several "trans-feminine" legends from Drucker's "chosen family" (Flawless Sabrina, Holly Woodlawn, Vaginal Davis), which debuted at the Hammer Museum in Los Angeles in 2012. They also took thousands of pictures of themselves and each other.

The photographs that make up "Relationship" were never meant for a mass audience; Drucker and Ernst didn't even share them with friends. They feel like small, private gifts for each other. One shows them topless and tenderly touching each other in bed, their faces flushed with the thrill of discovery. Another finds them nuzzling in the dark corner of what looks like a party, their eyes closed. Often Drucker or Ernst seem to be posing for the other, preening before a mirror or gazing directly at the camera.

These photos capture them as they figure out how to present their evolving selves. Ernst is often seen gazing in the distance, steely and remote, his face sprouting new facial hair. Drucker drapes herself across the bed, feline, come-hither and increasingly curvy. Their disdain for the "prurience" of public curiosity about trans bodies mean there are no full nudes in the book. Both lament that trans people are regularly asked about their genitals. "Cis people are not asked about their genitals, so it's a bit of a double standard," Drucker says. But the photos include some comic nods. One shows Ernst with two brown eggs between his legs; another has him eating a long link of sausage impaled on a fork. Drucker is seen holding a peeled grapefruit in her lap.

As a series, these photos trace a period in Drucker's and Ernst's lives when they were both undergoing profound personal changes. Yet they found something still and stable in each other. "That body of work really speaks to how much love and support can still be at the core of something that might seem unstable or uncertain or unfamiliar," says Stuart Comer, a co-curator of the 2014 Whitney Biennial. Comer is largely responsible for making these images public. Impressed by their film "She Gone Rogue" and excited by the energy and identity politics of many trans artists, he visited Drucker and Ernst in their Los Angeles studio in 2013. Over margaritas, they shared some of their personal snapshots. Comer was so moved by them that he asked to include a selection in the Biennial.

"The formula is so simple, but the cumulative effect of the series is extremely powerful," says Comer, who is now the chief curator of media and performance art at the Museum of Modern Art in New York. Unlike Drucker and Ernst's other collaborations, which tend to be more layered and complex, "Relationship" speaks to audiences because it is so direct. It is about love between two humans who happen to be trans.

"It's an earth-shattering book," says Kate Bornstein, a trans activist and queer theorist. "You can't read this book and not understand that trans is an identity that is desirable and filled with desire. There are going to be people writing to Zackary and Rhys saying, 'Oh, my God, thank you!' Because right now, being attracted to a trans person is seen as a perversion."

Drucker and Ernst understand why people are curious about them. "Trans people are basically asking everyone to re-evaluate their notions of gender," Drucker says. This involves more than changing a few names and pronouns. It means upending our rules about who gets to be a man or a woman, and how we expect everyone to behave. The effects can be disorienting. As someone who has occasionally chafed against the ways women are expected to perform femininity, I found myself marveling at Drucker's girlishness, including her perfectly painted fingernails (against my own hang-nailed nubs). What, I asked her, inspires these choices? Were they not burdensome? Drucker patiently explained that she does what makes her feel confident, and she likes the look of manicured nails. It was an answer that could have come from my mother.

Recognizing the difference between how gender is felt and how it is enforced can also be liberating. "Modern masculinity is so confining," Jerid Bartow, Drucker's cis-male boyfriend, told me one evening. "We're trained to swallow our emotions, to not seem like a sissy. But those expectations don't exist in our relationship, which is such a relief." Bartow recalled a night I was with him and Drucker while they were getting ready for a party, when he declared, "I'm having a clothing crisis!" next to a bed of discarded outfits. "That's something men are trained not to say."

Ernst points out that maleness does indeed come with privileges, like being able to ask for things unapologetically and say things authoritatively without being judged. But, he says, "effeminate men, gay men, smaller men, people who are perceived as younger men," don't enjoy quite the same benefits. As a 5-foot-9, sparsely bearded trans man who now identifies as gay, he says he has found it harder to secure a strong place in this "incredible pecking order." He adds that men who believe they are in male-only spaces will say "repulsive things about women." He suspects that this misogynistic posturing is largely about earning the respect of other men. "It's this male obsession with each other that results in a kind of weird, sort of insecure butt-sniffing."

Both Drucker and Ernst have made a commitment — separately and together — to live their lives as openly and proudly as possible. "As an artist, I've always believed in having a fully integrated self and not omitting parts of who you are or what your history is," Drucker says. "And being a woman named Zackary makes me very visible." Being out is not always easy. Like most trans men, Ernst passes as a cis male, so telling people he's trans means "rocking that boat every day." He recalls his discomfort during the Q.&A. sessions after screenings of his CalArts thesis short, "The Thing," at Sundance in 2012. The film is about a heterosexual couple on a fraught road trip. The man is trans. Audience members naturally asked him why he made that choice. "I realized I had to come out as trans every time on the stage," Ernst remembers. "You have to muster all this bravery and courage to transition and tell the whole world, and then you think, 'O.K., good, that's over.' But then you realize you have to continue that every day — forever."

**EMILY BOBROW** is a writer based in New York. Her work has appeared in The New York Times Book Review, The Believer and The Economist, where she was on the staff for 15 years.

# After Orlando, a Political
# Divide on Gay Rights Still Stands

BY JEREMY W. PETERS AND LIZETTE ALVAREZ  |  JUNE 15, 2016

WASHINGTON — For a fleeting moment this week, it seemed as if the massacre in Orlando, Fla., was having the unlikely and unintended impact of helping to bridge the chasm between Republicans and many in the gay community.

Mitt Romney offered "a special prayer for the L.G.B.T. community" after he learned of the attack. Senator Marco Rubio of Florida granted an interview to The Advocate, the gay news magazine, and expressed outrage at the Islamic State's persecution of gays. And Donald J. Trump repeatedly expressed solidarity with gay, lesbian, bisexual and transgender people, declaring, "I will fight for you" — an

SAM HODGSON FOR THE NEW YORK TIMES

From left, Police Chief John Mina and Gov. Rick Scott of Florida, far right, before a news conference outside Pulse, the club where the shootings took place.

unprecedented show of support from a presumptive Republican presidential nominee.

But the deep divide over gay rights remains one of the most contentious in American politics. And the murder of 49 people in an Orlando gay club has, in many cases, only exacerbated the anger from Democrats and supporters of gay causes, who are insisting that no amount of warm words or reassuring Twitter posts change the fact that Republicans continue to pursue policies that would limit legal protections for gays and lesbians.

In the weeks leading up to the killings, they pointed out, issues involving gays were boiling over in Congress and in Republican-controlled states around the country. More than 150 pieces of legislation were pending in state legislatures that would restrict rights or legal protections for sexual minorities. A Republican congressman read his colleagues a Bible verse from Romans that calls for the execution of gays. Congress was considering a bill that would allow individuals and businesses to refuse service to gay and lesbian couples.

North Carolina is facing a harsh backlash because of a law curtailing antidiscrimination protections for gays and requiring transgender people to use bathrooms that match the gender on their birth certificates. Mississippi's governor signed a similar bill.

Gays have surpassed Jews as the minority group most often targeted in hate crimes, according to the F.B.I.

The agitated reactions are just some of the ways identity politics have overtaken the tragedy in Orlando, with its combustible mix of issues that have long divided Americans: guns, gays, God and immigration.

"If one more Republican tells me they have gay friends, I'm gonna scream," said Representative Sean Patrick Maloney, Democrat of New York and one of just a few openly gay, lesbian or bisexual members of Congress. "I don't care that they have gay friends. I care that they're voting against equality."

The massacre, with stunning speed, has been transformed into a political wedge, beginning with fierce disagreements over just what the crime should be called. An attack by "radical Islamic terrorists," as Republicans insisted? A hate crime in a place seen as a safe haven by gays, as many Democrats said?

Politics have taken over in Washington and with particular force in Florida, where gay rights divisions are surfacing, Democrats are calling for gun controls in one of the most ardently pro-gun states, and Mr. Rubio, citing the events in Orlando, said he was reconsidering his decision not to seek re-election for his Senate seat.

One of the most bitter manifestations of the lingering animus happened in the shadow of the massacre scene itself when CNN's Anderson Cooper berated Florida's Republican attorney general, Pam Bondi, for speaking so affectionately about the dead while also being an unflinching opponent of efforts in her state to legalize same-sex marriage.

"Do you really think you are a champion of the gay community?" he asked her in an interview on Tuesday.

Ms. Bondi, who appeared rattled and caught off guard, accused Mr. Cooper on Wednesday of "creating more anger and havoc and hatred."

Amid the political sniping, a profound sense of fatigue was building — a familiar coda to many mass shootings.

"I'm not doing any of the political stuff," said Mayor Buddy Dyer of Orlando, a Democrat who has been praised for his handling of the crisis. "It's sad that on the national level they can't just focus on what they really need to focus on."

Because the killings have ignited debates on so many sensitive topics, there are many different opinions about what the focus should be. Democratic state lawmakers in Florida, led by State Senator Darren Soto, who is running for Congress, called for a special session on gun control here, a hard sell in a place known as the "Gunshine State." They also proposed a bill in the State Legislature that would ban people on the terrorist watch list or the no-fly list from buying guns, similar to efforts by Democrats in Washington.

But this week Gov. Rick Scott, a Republican, stressed that it was radical Islam that needed to be controlled, not guns. "The Second Amendment didn't kill anybody," Mr. Scott said. "Evil, radical Islam, ISIS — they killed."

Republicans and Democrats could not even agree on how to describe the attack. Mr. Scott was criticized for failing to mention, in numerous public appearances and interviews, that the victims were apparently targeted for their sexual identities. (He finally did on Wednesday, offering that the Orlando incident was "a clear attack on the gay and Hispanic community.") Representative Pete Sessions of Texas told a reporter on Tuesday that Pulse, where the attack occurred, "was a young person's club," not a gay club. His office later said he misunderstood.

The speaker of the House, Paul D. Ryan, made no mention of gays in his initial statement. Nor did the Senate majority leader, Mitch McConnell, who did note that the Islamic State beheaded women and crucified children.

Representative Rick W. Allen of Georgia, the Republican who last month read the Romans verse that says of homosexuals "they which commit such things are worthy of death" as the House was about to vote on a gay rights amendment, has not apologized. His spokeswoman did not respond to requests for comment on Wednesday.

"We aren't demanding that Republican lawmakers genuflect at the altar of the almighty gay agenda," said Kirk Fordham, a former senior Republican aide on Capitol Hill who has worked on gay rights causes. "Just acknowledge the discrimination and violence directed at us as a group. And sadly some Republican lawmakers think that is nonexistent or wildly exaggerated."

In Florida, activists noted that the state was still a place where gay and lesbian people could "get married on a Friday and fired on a Monday" because of inadequate nondiscrimination laws, in the words of Mallory Garner-Wells, the public policy director for Equality Florida.

"We've been trying to convey to people there's still a lot of work to do," she added. "Maybe this will be a wake-up call."

**JEREMY W. PETERS** reported from Washington, and **LIZETTE ALVAREZ** from Orlando, Fla.

# The Scope of the Orlando Carnage

OPINION | BY FRANK BRUNI | JUNE 12, 2016

THESE LOCATIONS ARE never random. These targets aren't accidental. They're the very vocabulary in which assailants like the Orlando gunman speak, and he chose a place where there's drinking. And dancing. And where L.G.B.T. people congregate, feeling a sense of welcome, of belonging.

That last detail is already in the foreground of the deadliest mass shooting in American history — and rightly so.

But let's be clear: This was no more an attack just on L.G.B.T. people than the bloodshed at the offices of Charlie Hebdo in Paris was an attack solely on satirists.

Both were attacks on freedom itself. Both took aim at societies that, at their best, integrate and celebrate diverse points of view, diverse systems of belief, diverse ways to love. And to speak of either massacre more narrowly than that is to miss the greater message, the more pervasive danger and the truest stakes.

We don't yet know all that much about Omar Mateen, who pulled the trigger, again and again, in a nightclub whose name connotes life, not death: Pulse. We'll be learning more in the hours and days to come, including just how potently homophobia in particular factored into his actions, how much ideological influence the Islamic State or other extremists had, how extensive his planning was, how far back he began plotting this, and how much he knew about Pulse itself and the specific composition of its crowd on different nights of the week.

But we can assume — no, we can be sure — that he was lashing out at an America at odds with his darker, smaller, more oppressive mindset. The people inside Pulse were citizens of it. More to the point, they were emblems of it. In Pulse they found a refuge. In Pulse they found joy. To him they deserved neither. And he communicated that with an assault rifle and bullets.

The Islamic State and its ilk are brutal to gay people, whom they treat in unthinkable ways. They throw gay people from rooftops. The footage is posted online. It's bloodcurdling, but it's not unique. In countries throughout the world, to be gay is to be in mortal danger. To embrace love is to court death.

That's crucial context for what happened in Orlando, and Orlando is an understandable prompt for questions about our own degrees of inclusion and fairness and whether we do all that we should to keep L.G.B.T. people safe. We don't.

As Florida Gov. Rick Scott spoke publicly of his heartache on Sunday, I saw complaints on social media about his own lack of support for issues important to L.G.B.T. people. Those complaints have merit.

But this isn't a moment for identity politics, which could muddle the significance of the carnage. Yes, that carnage exposed the special vulnerability of L.G.B.T. Americans to violent extremists, recommending special levels of security.

And there was a frightening coda to it on the opposite coast, in the Los Angeles area, where a man with an arsenal of weapons was arrested en route to gay pride festivities.

But the threat isn't only to L.G.B.T. Americans, as past acts of terror have shown and as everyone today must recognize. All Americans are under attack, and not exclusively because of whom we drink, dance or sleep with, but because of our bedrock belief that we should not be subservient to any one ideology or any one religion. That offends and inflames the zealots of the world.

Often our politicians can't find their voices. Sometimes their words are poignantly right.

President Obama, speaking about the victims on Sunday afternoon, said: "The place where they were attacked is more than a nightclub. It is a place of solidarity and empowerment where people have come together to raise awareness, to speak their minds and to advocate for their civil rights. So this is a sobering reminder that attacks on any American, regardless of race, ethnicity, religion or sexual orientation, is an attack on all of us and on the fundamental values of equality and dignity that define us as a country."

And this was Eric Garcetti, the Los Angeles mayor, at a news conference: "Today we know that we are targeted as Americans, because this is a society where we love broadly and openly, because we have Jews and Christians and Muslims and atheists and Buddhists marching together, because we are white, black, brown, Asian, Native American. The whole spectrum and every hue and every culture is here."

It was a perfect description of the country I love.

And it was an equally perfect description of what the Orlando gunman couldn't bear.

**FRANK BRUNI** is an Op-Ed columnist at The New York Times.

# Feminism Lost. Now What?

OPINION | BY SUSAN CHIRA | DEC 30, 2016

THIS WAS SUPPOSED to be the year of triumph for American women.

A year that would cap an arc of progress: Seneca Falls, 1848. The 19th Amendment, 1920. The first female American president, 2017. An inauguration that would usher in a triumvirate of women running major Western democracies. Little girls getting to see a woman in the White House.

Instead, for those at the forefront of the women's movement, there is despair, division and defiance. Hillary Clinton's loss was feminism's, too.

A man whose behavior toward women is a throwback to pre-feminist days is now setting the tone for the country. The cabinet that Donald J. Trump has nominated includes men — and a few women — with public records hostile to a range of issues at the heart of the women's movement. A majority of white women voted for him, shattering myths of female solidarity and the belief that demeaning women would make a politician unelectable.

More broadly, there is a fear that women's issues as the movement has defined them — reproductive rights, women's health, workplace advancement and the fight against sexual harassment, among others — could be trampled or ignored.

The Women's March on Washington on Jan. 21 is an apt metaphor for the moment: movement as primal scream. It grew out of a post on Facebook, was unconnected to any established women's organization, and has no set list of demands. Hundreds of thousands of women say they are going, but will their anger turn into a broader movement?

"We need a 'come to Jesus' moment," said C. Nicole Mason of the Center for Research and Policy in the Public Interest at the New York Women's Foundation. "I feel like the denial is very severe."

In the weeks after the election, in conversations with nearly two dozen advocates for women, I heard the fractures of a movement still regrouping after an unexpected defeat. They know that Mrs. Clinton didn't stand for the feminist movement directly, and that you could vote against her without saying you were voting against feminism. But one of the movement's goals was shattering that ultimate glass ceiling. Some say the failure to do so was so devastating that now is the time to rebuild from the ground up. Others insist it's time to stay the course.

The challenges are a proxy for the questions the Democratic Party must face over class, race, identity politics and tactics. The women's movement must balance how to broaden its message without losing its base. Courting the white working class could alienate black women still smarting over white women voting for a man whom many saw as racist — a choice that seemed to put racial identity over gender solidarity. Some younger women shun the feminist label altogether. It's not clear how far the tent can stretch without leaving some outside.

The overall struggle is to stay relevant in the age of Trump. "Before the election, even I was stunned by the sheer number of people I knew who came forward saying they'd been survivors of sexual assault," said Vivien Labaton, co-executive director of Make It Work, which promotes working families' economic security. "It's amazing to me the lightning speed at which these issues have receded. The story is the total omission of women. Overnight."

Many veterans of the women's movement bristle at the thought that the election was a rejection of feminism. Hillary Clinton won the popular vote by the largest recorded margin for a defeated candidate and won the majority of all women's votes. Eleanor Smeal, president of the Feminist Majority Foundation, cites a poll commissioned from Lake Research Partners conducted on the eve of the election. It found that 59 percent of women voters over all, and 59 percent of younger women, identify as feminists, up from 2012.

Heather Booth, long active in the movement, notes that polls consistently show majority support for child care, equal pay, prohibitions against sexual discrimination and the right to abortion. Ms. Smeal's and many other groups have reported intensified mobilization, donations and volunteerism after the election. For many, the defeat may well be an awakening, a visible sign of barriers they thought had been swept away.

But this consensus masks real struggles.

Although exit polls suggest that a majority of young women voted for Mrs. Clinton, their enthusiasm for Bernie Sanders during the primary seemed to say that for some, feminism's traditional preoccupations seem out of date.

In late October, when the polls indicated that Mrs. Clinton would win, I sought out young women to talk about their perceptions of her. Jessica Salans, 27, who is running for local office in Los Angeles in 2017, said she found Mrs. Clinton's feminism outdated, failing to prioritize climate change, income inequality and the toll of American intervention overseas.

"I saw a great documentary about the second-wave feminist movement, and it made me realize why people like Gloria Steinem were coming out in support of Hillary Clinton," she said. The brand of feminism that spoke to her, though, wasn't about breaking historic barriers. It was more specific: "progressive feminism, eco-feminism."

To many inside and outside the feminist movement, the Clinton campaign message missed the mark.

"White working-class women saw Hillary Clinton as another privileged white woman wanting to break the glass ceiling," said Joan C. Williams, professor at University of California Hastings College of the Law. "That metaphor makes sense if your central goal is to gain access to jobs that privileged men have. Hillary's feminism was not about them."

Feminism, which at its heart should mean opportunities for women in every sphere, has also come to be seen as a proxy for liberalism, alienating conservatives.

S. E. Cupp, a columnist for The Daily News in New York and a conservative who did not vote for Mr. Trump, said: "There's a condescension that comes across from some in the women's movement. There's this idea that if you're not liberal, you're a traitor to your gender. Is our message alienating entire groups of people, including women?"

She raised the provocative possibility that many women believed that Mr. Trump would keep the country safe in part because of his paternalistic, alpha male persona — and that was an implicit rejection of feminism's attempts to redefine gender roles.

Others worry that the women's movement has spent too much time policing language and behavior, blaming and shaming at the expense of dialogue. That, Professor Williams argues, can make misogyny attractive to the white working class, a way to rebel against condescending elites.

The answer, some argue, is rebranding feminism — recasting issues in economic terms relevant to the working class, men as well as women.

"While the working families agenda is very strong, it's not big enough to get the country back on its feet," said Celinda Lake, a long-time Democratic pollster. "It needs to be embedded in a bigger economic message. Sometimes we talk about it in ways that make it sound like it's just for women, to the exclusion of men."

By contrast, she said, Mr. Trump's economic platform was clear and compelling. Mrs. Clinton's calls for equal pay, child care, paid family leave and health insurance that covered birth control and mammograms, paled before the appeal of someone who promised to bring back better-paying manufacturing jobs and restore a lost standard of living.

The key is to link the two messages, to take issues that benefit women and show how they help families as a whole.

Ms. Lake described a focus group on equal pay she conducted with white union members in Michigan. She found that men were enthusiastic if they connected it with their own economic security. "One guy said, 'If the little lady doesn't get paid the same as I do, I need to get overtime and there's no OT anymore.' " The other men in the room, she said, agreed with him.

Men may also be more receptive when the message is applied to their daughters. Reshma Saujani runs the group Girls Who Code, aimed at preparing girls for careers in technology. She noted that when her organization tried to persuade parents to enroll their girls, abstract appeals to gender equity fell flat. Evoking fathers' dreams for their daughters had more resonance.

"You've lost your home but your daughter has a shot at going back up to the middle class," she said, explaining why that kind of pitch succeeded. "We have to talk to different parts of the country differently. We can't make the same gender arguments — it doesn't work."

In these postelection conversations, the rawest wounds were expressed by black women who felt betrayed by white women's support for Mr. Trump. These women worry that the national chest-beating about identity politics and the resolve to win back the white working class will come at their expense, subordinating issues of racial justice.

"You blame the people who voted for him, not the ones who didn't," said Salamishah Tillet, an associate professor of English and Africana studies at the University of Pennsylvania.

Early organizers of the women's march faced scorn for initially failing to include minority women in leadership positions, then drew fire for the original name of the event — Million Woman March — which appropriated the name of a march by black women in 1997.

"Ashes to ashes, dust to white liberal feminism," wrote LeRhonda Manigault-Bryant, associate professor of Africana studies at Williams College, in an impassioned open letter noting that white feminists now shared the kind of fears long known to black women.

Rather than playing down race, these women argue it's essential to recognize its interconnection with feminism. Allowing racism to fester, they say, threatens not only black women but also white women, because it encourages white nationalism, which is also hostile to women's rights.

But building bridges across racial and ethnic lines requires white feminists to understand that their experience is not universal, Professor Manigault-Bryant said. And it means defining women's issues as broadly as possible.

One of the paradoxes of 2016 was that some referendums on issues dear to the women's movement passed on the local level, from tax increases to expand child care programs in Ohio to raising the minimum wage in four states. Advocates see opportunities in localities, a key battleground. The Michigan People's Campaign focused on a statehouse district called Downriver Detroit, dispatching campaigners door to door to talk across party lines about issues like caring for the elderly, disabled relatives and children. Their progressive candidate won the local election, although Mr. Trump carried the same district.

Others see ballot initiatives as a potent weapon. "Maybe this moment was tailor-made for ballot measures as a critical form of policy making and protest," said Justine Sarver, executive director of the Ballot Initiative Strategy Center. The center conducted polling in 11 states and found wide support for issues like equal pay, child care, paid family leave and higher wages, and is gearing up for the 2018 midterm elections.

In the end, it's hard to argue that this election over all was a vote for the subordination of women. But it's a warning that feminism, as it has been defined, did not inspire enough people in enough places around the country. You didn't hear explicit calls for women to stay at home or be subservient to men, although it's an open question how many Americans are receptive to questioning traditional gender roles. Many who care about the place of women in American society are gripped by fears that men will now feel they have a free pass to demean women at home or in the workplace, that women's health, economic security and reproductive rights will be dealt severe blows.

Talking to women who voted for Mr. Trump, I found many who were working, divorced or single, opinionated and outspoken. They saw Hillary Clinton as a menace and Donald Trump as an agent of change, if a flawed one. Many were living what might be called liberated lives.

The challenge for the women's movement is to persuade more of the electorate that feminism is not merely a luxury for the privileged or the province only of liberals, but rather that it is essential to the freedom of every woman — and to her choices.

**SUSAN CHIRA** is a senior correspondent and editor on gender issues for The New York Times.

# I'm a White Man. Hear Me Out.

OPINION | BY FRANK BRUNI | AUG. 12, 2017

I'M A WHITE MAN, so you should listen to absolutely nothing I say, at least on matters of social justice. I have no standing. No way to relate. My color and gender nullify me, and it gets worse: I grew up in the suburbs. Dad made six figures. We had a backyard pool. From the 10th through 12th grades, I attended private school. So the only proper way for me to check my privilege is to realize that it blinds me to others' struggles and should gag me during discussions about the right responses to them.

But wait. I'm gay. And I mean gay from a different, darker day. In that pool and at that school, I sometimes quaked inside, fearful of what my future held. Back then — the 1970s — gay stereotypes went unchallenged, gay jokes drew hearty laughter and exponentially more Americans were closeted than out. We conducted our lives in whispers. Then AIDS spread, and we wore scarlet letters as we marched into the public square to plead with President Ronald Reagan for help. Our rallying cry, "silence = death," defined marginalization as well as any words could.

So where does that leave me? Who does that make me? Oppressor or oppressed? Villain or victim? And does my legitimacy hinge on the answer?

To listen to some of the guardians of purity on the left, yes.

Not long ago I wrote about Evergreen State College, which was roiled by protests after a white biology professor, Bret Weinstein, disparaged the particular tack of a day of racial healing. He raised valid points, only to be branded a bigot and threatened with violence.

That reception was wrong. I said so. And a reader responded: "I don't need one more white male criticizing young people of color." Other readers also homed in on my race — or on the professor's: "Weinstein will be fine. He's white." That automatically and axiomatically made him a less compelling actor in the drama, a less deserving object of concern, no matter his actions, no matter his argument.

Mark Lilla, a Columbia University professor, got a big, bitter taste of this late last year when he wrote, in The Times, about the presidential election and "identity politics," which, he argued, had hurt the Democratic Party. He maintained that too intense a focus on each minority group's discrete persecution comes at the expense of a larger, unifying vision.

Many people disagreed. Good. But what too many took issue with was, well, his identity. "White men: stop telling me about my experiences!" someone later scrawled on a poster that was put up to advertise a talk, "Identity Is Not Politics," that he gave at Wellesley College.

"But I wasn't talking about their experience or my experience," Lilla pointed out when I spoke with him recently. "I was talking about an issue."

In a new book coming out this week, "The Once and Future Liberal," he asserts that "classroom conversations that once might have begun, I think A, and here is my argument, now take the form, Speaking as an X, I am offended that you claim B. This makes perfect sense if you believe that identity determines everything. It means that there is no impartial space for dialogue. White men have one 'epistemology,' black women have another. So what remains to be said?"

And where are the bridges?

Race, gender, sexual orientation, class: All of this informs — and very often warps — how we see the world. And for much too long, this country's narrative has been scripted by white men, who have also dominated its stage and made its rules. Our advantage, as a class, is real and unearned.

The "check your privilege" exhortation asks us, rightly, to recognize that. It's about "being aware of systemic injustice and systemic inequality," Phoebe Maltz Bovy, the author of the recently published book "The Perils of 'Privilege,' " told me. And she applauds that.

But she worries that awareness disclaimers and privilege apologies have ferried us to a silly, self-involved realm of oppression Olympics. They promote the idea that people occupying different rungs of privilege or victimization can't possibly grasp life elsewhere on the ladder.

In her book she mocks the inevitable juncture in a certain kind of essay "where the writer (probably a cis White Lady, probably straight or bisexual, probably living in Brooklyn, definitely well educated, but not necessarily well-off) interrupts the usually scheduled programming to duly note that the issues she's describing may not apply to a trans woman in Papua New Guinea."

Should we really have say and sway only over matters that neatly dovetail with the category that we've been assigned (or assigned ourselves)? Is that the limit of our insights and empathies? During the Democratic primary, a Hillary Clinton supporter I know was told that he could not credibly defend her against charges of racism for her past use of the word "superpredators" because he's white.

That kind of thinking fosters estrangement instead of connection. Lilla noted that what people in a given victim group sometimes seem to be saying is: "You must understand my experience, and you can't understand my experience."

"They argue both, so people shrug their shoulders and walk away," he said.

Across a range of American institutions, we need more diversity. We need it to expunge and guard against the injustice that Bovy mentioned, and we need it because it's indeed a portal to broader knowledge and greater enlightenment. That means that white people — men in particular, even Google engineers — must make room in that narrative and space on that stage.

But I question the wisdom of turning categories into credentials when it comes to politics and public debate. I reject the assumptions — otherwise known as prejudices — that certain life circumstances prohibit sensitivity and sound judgment while other conditions guarantee them. That appraises the packaging more than it does the content. It ignores the complexity of people. It's reductive.

Thomas Chatterton Williams, the author of the memoir "Losing My Cool: Love, Literature, and a Black Man's Escape From the Crowd," got at this in an essay about privilege that he published last year, writing: "My black father, born in 1937 in segregated Texas, is an exponentially more worldly man than my maternal white Protestant grandfather, whose racism always struck me more as a sad function of his provincialism or powerlessness than anything else. I don't mean to excuse the corrosive effects of his view; I simply wish to note that when I compare these two men, I do not recognize my father as the victim."

At the beginning of this column I shared the sorts of personal details that register most strongly with those Americans who tuck each of us into some hierarchy of blessedness and affliction. So you know some important things about me, but not the most important ones: how I responded to the random challenges on my path, who I met along the way, what I learned from them, the degree of curiosity I mustered and the values that I honed as a result.

Those construct my character, and shape my voice, to be embraced or dismissed on its own merits. My gayness no more redeems me than my whiteness disqualifies me. And neither, I hope, defines me.

**FRANK BRUNI** is an Op-Ed columnist for The New York Times.

# Glossary

**affirmative action**  An action or policy whose purpose is to favor or help those people who suffer from discrimination.

**alt-right**  A vague and controversial term for a white nationalist movement whose members reject traditional conservatism and follow anti-Semitic, neo-fascist and other far-right hate groups.

**bigotry**  Intolerance toward those who hold different opinions than oneself.

**cultural appropriation**  The adoption of cultural items or artifacts from a minority culture by a dominant culture. The term and its use has become controversial both among conserative and liberal groups.

**diversity**  A range of different things, including identities; the state of being different.

**dominant**  The most important or powerful thing, idea or group; dominant culture refers to the culture that wields the most influence around the globe or in a particular society.

**fascism**  An authoritarian regime that places the importance of the nation and race above the importance of individual citizens.

**feminism**  A movement based on or the belief that women are equal to men and deserve equal protections under the law.

**globalization**  The process in which people around the world become more interconnected; this is largely tied with the growth and influence of multinational companies and the free market.

**ideology**  A system of ideas; usually the foundation of belief that leads to economic and political policy.

**implicit**  Implied but not fully expressed; not obvious or explicit.

**liberalism** A political and economic ideology that generally supports democracy, equal rights and free markets; liberalism is linked with a focus on the individual in political systems, rather than on the majority.

**marginalization** The treatment of a person or a group of people as unimportant or marginal.

**micro-aggressions** Indirect, small or unintentional aggressions toward a person or group of people in a marginalized group.

**misogyny** The dislike of and prejudice toward women.

**multiculturalism** The presence of or support for multiple cultures and cultural identities within a society.

**nationalism** A political and economic system in which the needs of that particular nation are considered foremost; also, patriotic feelings or actions toward one's homeland.

**partisanship** Bias or prejudice toward a particular cause; especially a sometimes blind allegiance toward a particular political party or cause.

**patriarchy** A political and social system in which males hold greater power than women.

**polarization** The division of groups into two or more factions that hold opposing beliefs.

**populism** A form of politics in which politicians cater to the needs and desires of ordinary people; in contemporary politics populism is associated with authoritarianism, in which politicians or the government appeal vaguely to the people in order to wield greater political power.

**privilege** A special right or advantage that only particular people or groups of people have.

**progressive** In politics, a person or party that favors social reform and liberal ideas.

**race-baiting** The making of verbal attacks against a group of people based on their race; a verbal expression of racism.

**resistance** The refusal to accept something; in politics, the refusal to agree with and the plan to act against a stated political agenda.

**tribalism** The state of being organized into tribes or groups; in a derogatory sense, the negative beliefs or attitudes that come from allegiance to one's own social, racial, religious or cultural group.

**trigger warning** A statement before a speech or other action that warns the audience of possible "triggers," or potentially distressing material.

**whitelash** In common terms, the backlash by racist white groups against civil rights advances.

**white nationalists** People who believe in white supremacy and that there is one national and racial identity that must be favored.

**white supremacy** A racial ideology based on the belief that white people are superior to other races.

# Media Literacy Terms

"Media literacy" refers to the ability to access, understand, critically assess and create media. The following terms are important components of media literacy, and they will help you critically engage with the articles in this title.

**angle**  The aspect of a news story that a journalist focuses on and develops.

**attribution**  The method by which a source is identified or by which facts and information are assigned to the person who provided them.

**balance**  Principle of journalism that both perspectives of an argument should be presented in a fair way.

**bias**  A disposition of prejudice in favor of a certain idea, person or perspective.

**byline**  Name of the writer, usually placed between the headline and the story.

**caption**  Identifying copy for a picture; also called a legend or cutline.

**chronological order**  Method of writing a story presenting the details of the story in the order in which they occurred.

**column**  A type of story that is a regular feature, often on a recurring topic, written by the same journalist, generally known as a columnist.

**commentary**  A type of story that is an expression of opinion on recent events by a journalist generally known as a commentator.

**credibility**  The quality of being trustworthy and believable, said of a journalistic source.

**critical review**  A type of story that describes an event or work of art, such as a theater performance, film, concert, book, restaurant, radio or television program, exhibition or musical piece, and offers critical assessment of its quality and reception.

**editorial**  Article of opinion or interpretation.

**fake news**  A fictional or made-up story presented in the style of a legitimate news story, intended to deceive readers; also commonly used to criticize legitimate news because of its perspective or unfavorable coverage of a subject.

**feature story**  Article designed to entertain as well as to inform.

**headline**  Type, usually 18 point or larger, used to introduce a story.

**human interest story**  A type of story that focuses on individuals and how events or issues affect their life, generally offering a sense of relatability to the reader.

**impartiality**  Principle of journalism that a story should not reflect a journalist's bias and should contain balance.

**intention**  The motive or reason behind something, such as the publication of a news story.

**interview story**  A type of story in which the facts are gathered primarily by interviewing another person or persons.

**motive**  The reason behind something, such as the publication of a news story or a source's perspective on an issue.

**news story**  An article or style of expository writing that reports news, generally in a straightforward fashion and without editorial comment.

**op-ed**  An opinion piece that reflects a prominent individual's opinion on a topic of interest.

**paraphrase**  The summary of an individual's words, with attribution, rather than a direct quotation of their exact words.

**quotation**  The use of an individual's exact words indicated by the use of quotation marks and proper attribution.

**reliability** The quality of being dependable and accurate, said of a journalistic source.

**rhetorical device** Technique in writing intending to persuade the reader or communicate a message from a certain perspective.

**source** The origin of the information reported in journalism.

**style** A distinctive use of language in writing or speech; also a news or publishing organization's rules for consistent use of language with regards to spelling, punctuation, typography and capitalization, usually regimented by a house style guide.

**tone** A manner of expression in writing or speech.

# Media Literacy Questions

**1.** "Identity Politics and Its Defenders" (on page 15) is an example of a critical review. What is the purpose of a critical review? Do you feel this article achieved that purpose?

**2.** Does Brendan Nyhan demonstrate the journalistic principle of impartiality in his article "Is the Slide Into Tribal Politics Inevitable?" (on page 35)? If so, how did he do so? If not, what could he have included to make his article more impartial?

**3.** What is the intention of the article "White Women Voted Trump. Now What?" (on page 39)? How effectively does it achieve its intended purpose?

**4.** Identify the various sources cited in the article "Why Americans Vote 'Against Their Interest': Partisanship" (on page 44). How does Amanda Taub attribute information to each of these sources in her article? How effective are the attributions in helping the reader identify the sources?

**5.** What type of story is "A Voice of Hate in America's Heartland" (on page 116)? Can you identify another article in this collection that is the same type of story?

**6.** In "The Great Political Divide Over American Identity" (on page 50), Lynn Vavreck paraphrases information from specific sources. What are the strengths of using a paraphrase as opposed to a direct quote? What are the weaknesses?

**7**. Compare the headlines of "The Pull of Racial Patronage" (on page 152) and "I'm a White Man. Hear Me Out." (on page 205). Which is a more compelling headline, and why? How could the less compelling headline be changed to better draw the reader's interest?

**8**. "The Stars of 'Black Panther' Waited a Lifetime for This Moment" (on page 94) is an example of an interview. Can you identify skills or techniques used by Reggie Ugwu to gather information from Chadwick Boseman, Ryan Coogler, Danai Gurira, Michael B. Jordan and Lupita Nyong'o?

**9**. "A Voice of Hate in America's Heartland" (on page 116) features several photographs. What do these photographs add to the article?

**10**. The article "We're All Fascists Now" (on page 160) is an example of an op-ed. Identify how Bari Weiss's attitude and tone help convey her opinion on the topic.

**11**. Which article collected here might be an example of a human interest story? Why?

# Citations

All citations in this list are formatted according to the Modern Language Association's (MLA) style guide.

**BOOK CITATION**

NEW YORK TIMES EDITORIAL STAFF, THE. *Identity Politics.* New York: New York Times Educational Publishing, 2019.

**ONLINE ARTICLE CITATIONS**

ALTER, ALEXANDRA. "With 'There There,' Tommy Orange Has Written a New Kind of American Epic." *The New York Times*, 31 May 2018, https://www.nytimes.com/2018/05/31/books/tommy-orange-there-there-native-american.html.

BLOW, CHARLES M. "Resistance, for the Win!" *The New York Times,* 9 Nov. 2017, https://www.nytimes.com/2017/11/09/opinion/resistance-trump-virginia-republicans.html.

BOBROW, EMILY. "How Two Producers of 'Transparent' Made Their Own Trans Lives More Visible." *The New York Times*, 18 Sept. 2016,://www.nytimes.com/2016/09/18/magazine/how-two-producers-of-transparent-are-making-trans-lives-more-visible-starting-with-their-own.html.

BROOKS, DAVID. "A Renaissance on the Right." *The New York Times*, 12 Apr. 2018, https://www.nytimes.com/2018/04/12/opinion/renaissance-right-gop.html.

BRUNI, FRANK. "I'm a White Man. Hear Me Out." *The New York Times*, 12 Aug. 2017, https://www.nytimes.com/2017/08/12/opinion/sunday/identity-politics-white-men.html.

BRUNI, FRANK. "The Scope of the Orlando Carnage." *The New York Times*, 13 Jun. 2016, https://www.nytimes.com/2016/06/13/opinion/the-scope-of-the-orlando-carnage.html.

CALDWELL, CHRISTOPHER. "What the Alt-Right Really Means." *The New York Times*, 2 Dec. 2016, https://www.nytimes.com/2016/12/02/opinion/sunday /what-the-alt-right-really-means.html.

CHIRA, SUSAN. "Feminism Lost. Now What?" *The New York Times*, 30 Dec. 2016, https://www.nytimes.com/2016/12/30/opinion/sunday/feminism-lost -now-what.html.

CHIRA, SUSAN, AND MATT FLEGENHEIMER. "Stacey Abrams Didn't Play It Safe. Neither Do These Female Candidates." *The New York Times*, 29 May 2018, https://www.nytimes.com/2018/05/29/us/politics/women-candidates -midterms.html.

DOUTHAT, ROSS. "The Pull of Racial Patronage." *The New York Times*, 17 Aug. 2016, https://www.nytimes.com/2016/08/17/opinion/campaign-stops/the -pull-of-racial-patronage.html.

DOWD, MAUREEN. "When Hillary Clinton Killed Feminism." *The New York Times*, 14 Feb. 2016, https://www.nytimes.com/2016/02/14/opinion/sunday /when-hillary-clinton-killed-feminism.html.

DYSON, MICHAEL ERIC. "What Donald Trump Doesn't Know About Black People." *The New York Times*, 17 Dec. 2016, https://www.nytimes.com /2016/12/17/opinion/sunday/what-donald-trump-doesnt-know-about -black-people.html.

FAUSSET, RICHARD. "A Voice of Hate in America's Heartland." *The New York Times*, 25 Nov. 2017, https://www.nytimes.com/2017/11/25/us/ohio -hovater-white-nationalist.html.

GREENIDGE, KAITLYN. "Who Gets to Write What?" *The New York Times*, 25 Sept. 2016, https://www.nytimes.com/2016/09/25/opinion/sunday/who -gets-to-write-what.html.

IVES, MIKE. "For Some Viewers, 'Crazy Rich Asians' Is Not Asian Enough." *The New York Times*, 16 Aug. 2018, https://www.nytimes.com/2018/08/16 /world/asia/crazy-rich-asians-cast-singapore.html.

KRISTOF, NICHOLAS. "Identity Politics and a Dad's Loss." *The New York Times*, 8 Dec. 2016, https://www.nytimes.com/2016/12/08/opinion/identity-politics -and-a-dads-loss.html.

KRUGMAN, PAUL. "The Populism Perplex." *The New York Times*, 25 Nov. 2016, https://www.nytimes.com/2016/11/25/opinion/the-populism-perplex.html.

LALAMI, LAILA. "The Identity Politics of Whiteness." *The New York Times*, 21 Nov. 2016, https://www.nytimes.com/2016/11/27/magazine/the-identity -politics-of-whiteness.html.

LEONHARDT, DAVID. " 'Identity Politics' and Its Defenders." *The New York Times*, 21 Nov. 2016, https://www.nytimes.com/2016/11/21/opinion /identity-politics-and-its-defenders.html.

LEONHARDT, DAVID. "Is All This Talk of Racism Bad for Democrats?" *The New York Times*, 16 Jan. 2018, https://www.nytimes.com/2018/01/16/opinion /trump-racisim-democrats.html.

LETT, PHOEBE. "White Women Voted Trump. Now What?" *The New York Times*, 10 Nov. 2016, https://www.nytimes.com/2016/11/10/opinion/white -women-voted-trump-now-what.html.

LILLA, MARK. "The End of Identity Liberalism." *The New York Times*, 18 Nov. 2016, https://www.nytimes.com/2016/11/20/opinion/sunday /the-end-of-identity-liberalism.html.

LYNCH, FREDERICK R. "Why Trump Supporters Distrust Immigration and Diversity." *The New York Times*, 4 Aug. 2017, https://www.nytimes .com/2017/08/04/opinion/trump-supporters-immigration-diversity.html.

MORRIS, WESLEY. " 'Bro-'Liferation." *The New York Times*, 20 Mar. 2016, https://www.nytimes.com/2016/03/20/magazine/bro-liferation.html.

NYHAN, BRENDAN. "Is the Slide Into Tribal Politics Inevitable?" *The New York Times*, 18 Nov. 2016, https://www.nytimes.com/2016/11/18/upshot/is-the -slide-into-pure-identity-politics-inevitable.html.

PETERS, JEREMY W., AND LIZETTE ALVAREZ. "After Orlando, a Political Divide on Gay Rights Still Stands." *The New York Times*, 15 Jun. 2016, https://www .nytimes.com/2016/06/16/us/after-orlando-a-political-divide-on-gay-rights -still-stands.html.

SEHGAL, PARUL. "How 'Privilege' Became a Provocation." *The New York Times*, 19 Jun. 2015, https://www.nytimes.com/2015/07/19/magazine /how-privilege-became-a-provocation.html.

SHRIVER, LIONEL. "Will the Left Survive the Millennials?" *The New York Times,* 23 Sept. 2016, https://www.nytimes.com/2016/09/23/opinion /will-the-left-survive-the-millennials.html.

SMARSH, SARAH. "Liberal Blind Spots Are Hiding the Truth About 'Trump Country.' " *The New York Times*, 19 July 2018, https://www.nytimes.com /2018/07/19/opinion/trump-corporations-white-working-class.html.

STACK, LIAM. "Alt-Right, Alt-Left, Antifa: A Glossary of Extremist Language." *The New York Times*, 15 Aug. 2017, https://www.nytimes.com/2017/08/15 /us/politics/alt-left-alt-right-glossary.html.

STEPHENS, BRET. "Free Speech and the Necessity of Discomfort." *The New*

*York Times*, 22 Feb. 2018, https://www.nytimes.com/2018/02/22/opinion /free-speech-discomfort.html.

SURO, ROBERTO. "The Real 'Trump Effect' for Young Latinos." *The New York Times*, 27 May 2018, https://www.nytimes.com/2016/05/29/opinion /campaign-stops/the-real-trump-effect-for-young-latinos.html.

TACKETT, MICHAEL, ET AL. "A Year After Trump, Women and Minorities Give Groundbreaking Wins to Democrats." *The New York Times,* 8 Nov. 2017, https://www.nytimes.com/2017/11/08/us/politics/democrats-women -minorities.html.

TAUB, AMANDA. "Behind 2016's Turmoil, a Crisis of White Identity." *The New York Times*, 2 Nov. 2016, https://www.nytimes.com/2016/11/02/world /americas/brexit-donald-trump-whites.html.

TAUB, AMANDA. "Why Americans Vote 'Against Their Interest': Partisanship." *The New York Times*, 12 Apr. 2017, https://www.nytimes.com/2017/04/12 /upshot/why-americans-vote-against-their-interest-partisanship.html.

UGWU, REGGIE. "The Stars of 'Black Panther' Waited a Lifetime for This Moment." *The New York Times*, 12 Feb. 2018, https://www.nytimes.com /2018/02/12/movies/black-panther-marvel-chadwick-boseman-ryan -coogler-lupita-nyongo.html.

VAVRECK, LYNN. "The Great Political Divide Over American Identity." *The New York Times*, 2 Aug. 2017, https://www.nytimes.com/2017/08/02/upshot /the-great-political-divide-over-american-identity.html.

WEISS, BARI. "We're All Fascists Now." *The New York Times*, 7 Mar. 2018, https://www.nytimes.com/2018/03/07/opinion/were-all-fascists-now.html.

WEST, LINDY. "We Got Rid of Some Bad Men. Now Let's Get Rid of Bad Movies." *The New York Times*, 3 Mar. 2018, https://www.nytimes.com /2018/03/03/opinion/sunday/we-got-rid-of-some-bad-men-now-lets-get-rid -of-bad-movies.html.

ZERNIKE, KATE. "Don't Run This Year': The Perils for Republican Women Facing a Flood of Resistance." *The New York Times,* 13 Aug. 2018, https:// www.nytimes.com/2018/08/13/us/politics/republican-women-candidates -midterms.html.

# Index

*This book is current up until the time of printing. For the most up-to-date reporting, visit www.nytimes.com.*